The Heroine's Journey Workbook

The Heroine's Journey Workbook

A MAP FOR EVERY WOMAN'S QUEST

Maureen Murdock

SHAMBHALA

Shambhala Publications, Inc.
2129 13th Street
Boulder, Colorado 80302
www.shambhala.com

Cover art by iStock
Cover and interior design by Kate E. White

9 8 7 6 5 4 3

Printed in the United States of America

♾ This edition is printed on acid-free paper that meets the American National Standards Institute Z39.48 Standard.
♻ This book is printed on 30% postconsumer recycled paper.
For more information please visit www.shambhala.com.
Shambhala Publications is distributed worldwide by Penguin Random House, Inc., and its subsidiaries.

THE LIBRARY OF CONGRESS CATALOGUES THE
PREVIOUS EDITION OF THIS BOOK AS FOLLOWS:
Murdock, Maureen. The heroine's journey workbook / by Maureen Murdock.
p.   cm.
Includes bibliographical references.
ISBN 1-57062-255-8 (pbk.: alk. paper)
ISBN 978-1-61180-831-5 (2020 reissue)
1. Women—Psychology.   2. Femininity.   3. Sex role.   I. Title.
HQ1206.M85   1998   97-42875
305.4—dc21   CIP

For my sister and dear friend
Rosemary

Contents

Acknowledgments

No heroine journeys alone. It always takes an array of allies and adversaries to make any perilous journey. Here I'll acknowledge my allies (some of whom also function as adversaries, as every good mythmaker knows!). Special thanks to my editor at Shambhala, Emily Hilburn Sell, who restored my faith in publishing and made me laugh; Susan King, who read most of the manuscript and encouraged me to meander when I was stuck; Anita Swanson and Saralie Liner, writers themselves, who gave suggestions about tone and content; Amber Copilow, who accompanied me on early-morning walks and mental wanderings; my daughter, Heather, for her insightful reading and comments; my son, Brendan, for understanding my highs and lows and sending me his own allies for support; and my editor, Margaret Ryan, for making the Bricklayer's Daughter laugh.

I also want to acknowledge the thousands of women and men, girls and boys who have journeyed with me in Heroine's Journey workshops, dream groups, teen groups, and writing classes over the past thirty years. Their intrepid journeys and their generous permission to use their stories and dreams inspired me to offer these exercises to more people.

Thanks to my workshop partner, the artist Valerie T. Bechtol, for sharing her notes on the spirit doll and maskmaking exercises that she created and her expertise in both, as well as to Flor Fernandez, Donna DeLuca, Elizabeth Waters, and Layne Redmond, who taught with me at Omega Institute. Thanks to Carol Pearson for teaching with me at Naropa. Thanks to Linda

Venis and Ray Montalvo at the UCLA Extension Writers' Program and to my colleagues Celeste Torrens, Terry Binkowitz, Nancee Redmond, and Leon and Linda Weber for their support. Thanks to Sally McKissick for proofreading the manuscript, to Victoria Wertheimer for her genius on computers, and to Nora Dvosin, Henry Murray, and Lewin Wertheimer for providing comic relief.

Thanks also to Elisa Cabal for her dreams, Charles Goodman for offering a clear mirror, Fernando Mata for his healing hands, Judith Stone for her wonderful perspective on life, and Lucien Wulsin, Jr., for being a catalyst. Many thanks to the poets and artists who gave generously of their time and talent to this book: Joanne Battiste, Tina Michelle Datsko, Marti Glenn, Fiona O'Connell, and Anna Pomaska.

Finally, my gratitude to the teachers who took me by the hand and pointed the way: Polly McVickar, Adelaide Fogg, Jean Houston, Joseph Campbell, and Thich Nhat Hanh.

The Heroine's Journey Workbook

Introduction

*The task for today's woman is to heal the wounding of the feminine
that exists deep within herself and the culture.*
—MAUREEN MURDOCK, *The Heroine's Journey*

Most of us spend our lifetime trying to tease meaning out of the circumstances of our lives. We search for meaning as we tell the story about how and where we grew up, who our parents were, how the significant people in our lives influenced us, what challenges and obstacles we faced, and how we dealt with triumph and failure. The story we tell ourselves and others gives us a sense of identity. It helps us organize our life in a way that gives it meaning and direction.

In adulthood, we look for maps or guidelines that give us clues about our development through the stages of life. We look at how the events of early childhood and adolescence influence the choices we make in adulthood, midlife, and elderhood. We look around us for mentors who are consciously navigating their own journeys. We search for a sense of belonging within our community; we wonder about our purpose and how we fit into the larger picture, and if there is, indeed, a larger picture.

Our personal myth—or story—provides a way for us to understand our origins, who we are, where we belong, and whether our life has meaning. If we can be aware of our own story as it unfolds, we have a better chance of understanding and making friends with our lives. Mythic patterns provide guidelines or maps. A personal myth is a constellation of beliefs, feelings, and images that is organized around a core theme and addresses one of the domains within which mythology traditionally functions. These are:

MEANING: the urge to comprehend the natural world in a
   meaningful way;
MAP: the search for a marked pathway through the succeeding
   epochs of human life;
TRIBE: the need to establish security and fulfilling relationships
   within a community; and
PLACE: the longing to know one's part in the vast wonder and
   mystery of the universe.

A personal myth asks why am I here, how do I make my way through life, what tribe do I belong to, and where do I fit in the greater scheme of things. A personal myth is not a set script in which we enact a role; our personal myth evolves over time. D. Stephenson Bond writes, "Over a lifetime we don't so much live out of a personal myth as live out the death and rebirth of a personal myth. We fall into and out of myth several times over the course of a lifetime. The core experience remains but over a lifetime must be worked and reworked."[1]

Gender, culture, economic background, and religious beliefs inform our personal mythology and the symbols and rites that carry our myth forward.

> One can perceive one's life as a story, unfolding in a spiraling series of experiences each having the three-phase form of separation/ordeal-learning process/return.
> —LINDA SUSSMAN

In a time when cultural myths about women and men are being challenged on every front and there is a political and religious impetus to return to scripts of the past, many people are searching for a deeper understanding of their own story. It is therefore important for us to look to ancient myths for wisdom and inspiration and to explore the patterns of ancient myth for possible direction.

The mythic pattern we will be exploring in this book is the journey of the heroine, the quest to heal the deep wounding of our feminine nature on a personal, cultural, and spiritual level. As women, we take a psycho-spiritual journey to become whole, integrating all parts of our nature. Sometimes this journey is conscious, but in many cases it is not.

I wrote *The Heroine's Journey* in 1990 to describe the stages of woman's experience of the mythic quest. I had spent years studying with and working with Joseph Campbell; his work with the journey of the hero inspired my desire to write something that was particular to the feminine journey. Since that time, I have received thousands of letters from women (and some men) all over the world asking for guidance in making the journey conscious. Hence, this workbook.

This journey begins with an initial separation from the feminine as the heroine separates from her mother and searches for an identity in a masculine-defined culture. She develops both masculine skills and allies to help her carve out her niche in a product-oriented, competitive environment. She puts on her armor, picks up her sword, chooses her swiftest steed, and goes into battle. Along the way, she travels the road of trials as she faces challenges to overcome the myths of female inferiority, dependency, and romantic love as she strives for the illusory boon of success—an advanced degree, a vested corporate position, relationship, money, political power—promised by the culture.

After making it in a man's world or becoming bloodied in an attempt to do so, the heroine experiences a deep feeling of spiritual aridity. She has achieved everything she set out to achieve and looks for the next hurdle to jump, the next promotion, the next relationship, filling every spare moment with *doing*. She begins to ask, "What is all of this for? I've achieved everything I've set out to achieve and I feel empty. What have I lost?" What she may have lost is a deep relationship to herself.

During the next part of the journey, the heroine goes through an initiation and descent to the goddess to reclaim the depths of her lost feminine soul. This stage may involve a seemingly endless period of wandering, grief, and rage, of looking for the lost pieces of herself and meeting the dark feminine. It may take weeks, months, or years, and for many it may involve a period of voluntary isolation (a period of silence) during which she learns to listen deeply to her soul. The heroine yearns to reconnect with her feminine nature and to heal the mother-daughter split, the wound that occurred with the initial rejection of the feminine. This may or may not involve an actual healing of the relationship between a woman and her personal mother. A healing does occur, however, within the woman herself as she begins to nurture her body and soul and reclaim her feelings, intuition, sexuality, creativity, and humor.

She then begins to identify the disowned, wounded parts of her masculine nature and finally learns to integrate and balance all aspects of her being. In this process, the heroine becomes a spiritual warrior. She must learn the delicate art of balance and have the patience for the slow, subtle integration of the feminine and masculine aspects of herself. She first hungers to lose her feminine self and to merge with the masculine, and once she has done this, she begins to realize that this is neither the answer nor the end. She must not discard nor give up what she has learned throughout her heroic quest, but must learn to view her hard-earned skills and successes not so much as the goal but as one part of the entire journey. She will then begin to use these skills to work toward the larger quest of bringing consciousness to others to preserve the balance of life on earth.

This journey, like the journey of the hero delineated by Joseph Campbell in *The Hero with a Thousand Faces,* describes the individuation process. Individuation refers to the lifelong process of becoming the complete human being we were meant to be. It reveals our special, *individual* nature.[2] Campbell

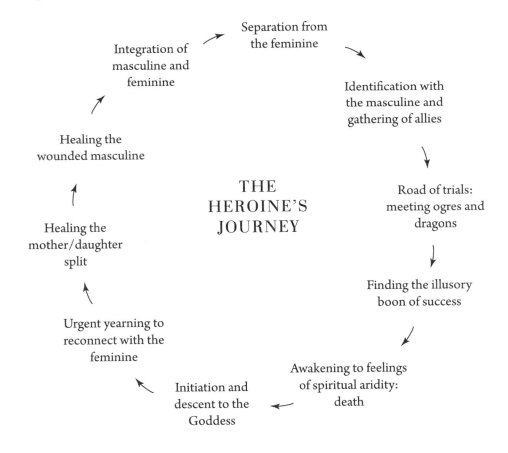

The heroine's journey begins with "Separation from the feminine"
and ends with "Integration of masculine and feminine."

explored this process through the stages of the myth of the hero, the journey of a man (or woman) who has been able to battle past his personal and local historical limitations to a new, emergent human form. The hero responds to a Call to Adventure, crosses the Threshold into unknown realms, meets Allies or supernatural guides who assist him in his journey, and confronts Adversaries or Threshold Guardians who try to block his progress. The hero then experiences an Initiation in the Belly of the Whale, a series of Trials that test his skills and resolve before he can find the treasure or Boon he seeks. He meets a mysterious partner in the form of a Goddess, enters into a Sacred Marriage, and embarks upon a Return journey across the threshold to bring back to the people the treasure he has found. This hero's journey is a search for the soul and is chronicled in mythologies and fairy tales throughout the world.

> *It has always been the prime function of mythology and rite to supply the symbols that carry the human spirit forward, in counteraction to those other constant human fantasies that tend to hold it back.*
> —JOSEPH CAMPBELL,
> *Primitive Mythology*

It is the familiar tale of the knight who hears that the king is in trouble, sharpens his sword, mounts his steed, and goes in search of lost treasure or knowledge to renew the kingdom. Along the way, he outwits ogres, slays dragons, finds the treasure, and falls in love with a beautiful maiden. He makes his way back to the kingdom with the boon of his success, restores the king, and, if he is lucky, gets to spend a weekend in bed with his lady love before taking off to slay another dragon. Variations on this pattern of the heroic quest have been lived out by countless men and women of all cultures and used as a blueprint by screenwriters and novelists alike to give the lives of their characters meaning. But it does not adequately describe the woman's journey, because our task at this time is to heal the deep wounding of the feminine within ourselves and in the culture.

I am what is called a father's daughter—a woman who has identified primarily with her father, oftentimes rejecting her mother; a woman who has sought attention and approval not only from her personal father but also from the culture at large by aspiring to succeed according to masculine values. The Heroine's Journey is described from the point of view of a father's daughter. Although not every woman reading this book is a father's daughter in relationship to her personal father, I agree with the Jungian analyst Marion Woodman when she writes that most of us are fathers' daughters in relation to the predominantly masculine culture in which we live.

The model presented here does not necessarily fit the experience of all women of all ages, nor is it limited only to women. It addresses the journeys of both genders. It describes the experience of many people who strive to be active and make a contribution in the world, but who also fear what our progress-oriented society has done to the human psyche and to the ecological balance of the planet. Movement through these stages is not linear; it is cyclic and will most likely be repeated many times during a person's lifetime. You might also find yourself working on more than one stage of development at a time. The Heroine's Journey is a continuous cycle of development, growth, and learning. You may find that some parts apply to you and others do not. Use part or all of it as a blueprint for your own development.

Before we begin to explore the stages of the Heroine's Journey in depth, however, we must address the changing definitions of heroism and how cultural myths have influenced our perceptions about ourselves as women. The role of heroine has entailed accomplishing great tasks at the risk of endangering one's safety, security, health, and relationships (think of Joan of Arc and Florence Nightingale). Women who were able to "do it all," "be all things to all people," were admired and applauded, if not economically rewarded. Their focus was on accomplishment and service—the more they did, the more tasks they crossed off their list, the more value they felt they earned. The model of the smartly dressed woman juggling briefcase and baby formula in courtrooms and boardrooms across the land became the goal of many young women, particularly in the 1970s and 1980s. A woman who did not achieve this type of external recognition and success often felt a deep sense of loss, or even failure.

The myth of female inferiority and dependency of the fifties and early sixties was traded for the myth of the superwoman of the eighties and nineties. Those women who sought political, economic, and spiritual equality with men in academia, business, and home felt an initial rush from their daily successes but eventually began to experience a weariness in their hearts. Burnout and divorce took a toll on their health, and the struggle for individual achievement lost its allure. With this shift, the definition of heroism demanded a change as well—from striving to satisfy the demands of the cacophony of outer voices to learning to balance personal, family, and professional lives and listen to the still voice within.

USING THIS BOOK

This workbook is written to guide you through the different stages of the Heroine's Journey. It will function much like the workshops I have conducted with women from ages thirteen to eighty-six throughout North America, Europe, and Mexico. It can be used with a group of women or by yourself. Together, we will explore each stage of the journey and look at the myths and fairy tales that illustrate these stages. The chapters include questions for you to consider about your development as a woman, as well as guided imagery, writing, and art exercises that will bring clarity and understanding to your journey. You may wish to purchase a special journal or notebook in which to do the writing and art exercises and record your dreams.

You may find it helpful to read the text of the entire book first to understand the path of the Heroine's Journey and then go back to explore the exercises in depth. Or you may choose to focus on one chapter at a time and work on the exercises in that chapter until you have completed them. Take your time with the exercises. Do them at your own pace and choose a time in which you will not be interrupted—you may want to schedule the same time each week.

You will find that the material suggested in the exercises serves as a springboard to evoke more memories, dreams, and insights. It is easy to become overwhelmed. You may wish to put the book down for a while and come back to it later. Movement through the stages is cyclic, and movement through the exercises is cyclic as well. Many issues will be examined at different levels throughout the book.

Work with the exercises sequentially or choose those within each chapter that you are most drawn to or most strongly resist. Most of us find that our greatest insights come from doing what we most strongly resist. Suggestions will be given about rituals you may wish to create to deepen the process.

It has been my experience that people who attend Heroine's Journey workshops get annoyed, judgmental, and angry on the third day, or whichever day we begin the descent. You may find that as you work with the descent material in chapter 3, you want to close the book and stop the process. Don't. Be kind to yourself and take a deep breath. Make yourself a cup of tea or go for a walk.

Support yourself with love and compassion. Never judge yourself. Be patient with your process and make a commitment to work through the issues inherent in the descent in your own timing. By doing so, I promise that you will curtail your stay in the underworld!

Awakenings require a woman to respond consciously, to accept the invitation to create herself anew, and to undertake the challenge no matter how frightened or inadequate she may feel. Thus each awakening call demands not only that it be heard, but that the woman find the courage to trust and affirm the call whenever it arises, wherever it takes her, and however much it challenges her way of being in the world.
—KATHLEEN NOBLE

You may want to share your insights with a friend or partner, or you may want to keep the entire experience private. That is your personal decision. As you read this book, feel free to underline passages, write notes to yourself, or doodle in the margins.

Your dreams will become an integral part of your journey, helping you to understand your own personal mythology. You can get a glimpse of mythic patterns in your dreams. Please record them either by pen or recorder and consider the wisdom they offer about your story and the challenges you are being given to support your soul's growth.

The basic function of dreams is to express the unconscious. The unconscious is the source of much of our thought, feeling, and behavior and has a powerful influence on us in ways we do not suspect. The unconscious communicates to our conscious mind through dreams and imagination.

Images in dreams should not be taken literally but seen as symbols of parts of yourself and dynamics within your inner life. Robert Johnson writes, "Dreams show us, in symbolic form, all the different personalities that interact within us and make up our total self."[3] Each character in your dream is an aspect of yourself revealing its own consciousness, desires, and point of view.[4]

Your dream symbols have a special individual meaning that belongs to you alone, just as the dream is ultimately yours. Pay attention to the personalities, symbols, and landscapes that repeat. Your unconscious is trying to get your attention. The point of recording your dreams and learning from them is to build consciousness. As you become versed in the symbols of your dream life, you will find hidden strengths and resources to help you on your journey. You may wish to acquaint yourself with books that provide an in-depth study of dreams: *Inner Work* by Robert A. Johnson and *Wisdom of the Heart* by Karen A. Signell are two excellent resources. Let us begin.

QUESTIONS FOR WRITING AND REFLECTION

Write your response to the following questions in your journal. Throughout the book, write as much or as little as you want in response to the questions and exercises. If you would prefer to speak your responses into a recorder so that you can listen to the sound of your own voice, please do so.

* Each one of us is a heroine. Who are the heroines in your life and how do you see yourself as heroic?
* As you look at the diagram of the Heroine's Journey on page 4, can you locate yourself? Are you exploring more than one stage at once?

GUIDED IMAGERY: LIFELINE

Before beginning this exercise and other guided imagery exercises in this workbook, gather your recorder or writing or art supplies to record your images after you have completed the visualization. You may wish to use journal or art pad, markers, crayons, pastels, or pens. You may also wish to play a recording of soothing music such as *Gymnosphere: Song of the Rose* by Jordan de la Sierra.

In this exercise you will look at the events of your childhood, adolescence, and early adulthood and see how your relationship to your body, mind, emotions, and spirit has influenced your life journey. Notice in particular what you have perceived as your strengths, skills, accomplishments, and innate gifts.

Be aware of how your position in the family influenced your actions and beliefs about yourself and how your relationship with each parent, sibling, and grandparent colored how you felt about yourself. Did the experience of divorce or a parent's death leave you in a position of authority or crippled by loss? What was your relationship to friends, teachers, and people in authority? Did an early illness or accident affect your perception of yourself? How did the gender assigned to you at birth, your culture, and your religious background influence your personal mythology?

Sit in a comfortable position and close your eyes. Begin to breathe in and out through your nostrils, giving yourself the suggestion that with each exhalation you become more and more relaxed. With each exhalation you move into deeper and deeper levels of consciousness, where more images and memories are accessible to you. Now take a deep breath . . . hold it . . . and relax your breath with a slight sigh. Good. Let's do that again. Take a deep breath . . . hold it . . . relax. Good. Again, take a deep breath . . . hold it . . . and relax. Good. Now breathe at your own rate and imagine, if you will, that you are moving back in time to sometime in your early childhood, perhaps the time when you were five years old.

Now, still with your eyes closed, look down at your five-year-old feet. Notice the color and style of your shoes. Notice whether you are wearing lace-up shoes, sandals, Mary Janes, or whether you are barefoot. Now, become aware of your five-year-old body, your legs, buttocks, pelvis, belly, chest, back, shoulders, arms and hands, your neck, face, and hair. How are you wearing your hair as a young child? Is it short, long, curly, straight? What color is it? Do you have braids or a ponytail? Become as aware of yourself at five as possible.

Now, become aware of the environment around you. Are you at home, in nature, in the city, by the seashore? Notice the colors, shapes, smells, tastes, and sounds in your environment. Perhaps you are with your family. Who are the important people in your life at this time? Do you have a sibling, a pet, a grandparent? Who are the people who appreciate you for who you are? What are you learning about yourself from how people respond to you?

Now, become aware of your skills at this time in your life. What are you learning to do? How are you being challenged mentally, artistically, and physically? What are you curious about? What do you appreciate about yourself? What do others appreciate about you? How do you feel about yourself as a girl?

What is your relationship to nature, your dreams, your intuition? Do you have a relationship to spirit as you define it—an angel, God, an imaginary friend?

Become as aware of yourself at five or some important time in your early childhood as you can. Pause for a minute or more. Now leave your five-year-old self, and we will gently move forward in time.

Look down now and see your ten-year-old feet. Become aware of the shoes you are wearing at ten. Notice their color and style. Become aware of your ten-year-old body—your legs, buttocks, pelvis, chest, back, shoulders, arms and hands, neck, face, and hair. How are you wearing your hair at ten? What clothes are you wearing? What skills are you learning with your body? How are you challenging yourself? What are you learning about your strength and stamina? How do you feel about your body, your sexuality?

Now, notice your environment. What are the colors, shapes, smells, tastes, and sounds in your environment? Who are the important people in your life now? Who are your friends? What do you do together? What is your relationship with your parents and family?

How do you feel about yourself at this time—self-confident, shy, outgoing, funny? What are you learning about yourself as a girl from the way others treat you?

How are you challenging your mind and what are you learning? What is your relationship to learning, to teachers, to your creativity? What are you curious about? What do you long for?

What is your relationship to spirit . . . to nature . . . to your community? Are you involved in religious study or your own spiritual rituals, and how does this nurture you? Become as aware as possible of your ten-year-old self. Pause one minute or more. Now, leave your ten-year-old self and we will gently move forward in time to your adolescence.

Now, look down and see your fifteen-year-old feet. Notice the color and style of your shoes or your bare feet. Become aware of your adolescent body, your buttocks, pelvic area, belly, chest and breasts, back, shoulders, arms, hands, neck, face, and hair. Notice how you are wearing your hair and what color it is. Are you wearing makeup? What style clothes are you wearing? Who are you dressing for? Notice how you feel about your body—have you started your period? How do you feel about your emerging sexuality? Do you have a boyfriend or a girlfriend? Do you have a secret crush on someone?

Become aware of your environment. What are the colors, shapes, smells, tastes, and sounds in your environment? What is the music you listen to? Who are the important people in your life now? Who are your friends? What do you do together? How do you spend your time? What is your relationship with your parents and family?

How are you challenging your mind and what are you learning about yourself both in school and out of school? Do you have a job, and what are you learning about money?

What is your relationship to teachers, coaches, to those in authority?

What is your relationship to sports and your creativity? What are you curious about? What do you long for? What are your goals for the future?

How do you feel about yourself at this time? What do people appreciate about you? What do you appreciate about yourself?

What is your relationship to spirit, to nature, to your own intuition? What is important to you about your community and your place in it?

Become as aware as possible of yourself as a teenager. Pause one minute. Now, leave your fifteen-year-old self and let's move forward in time to your early twenties.

Look down at the shoes you are wearing sometime in your early twenties. Notice their color and style. Become aware of your body in your early twenties—your legs, buttocks, pelvis, chest, breasts, back, shoulders, arms, hands, neck, face, and hair. How are you wearing your hair at this time? What color is it? What clothes are you wearing, and how do your clothes or jewelry reflect your role at this time in your life? What impression are you trying to convey? Are you a student, wife, mother, an artist? Are you working? traveling? Are you responsible for yourself economically?

Notice your environment. What are the colors, shapes, smells, tastes, and sounds in your environment? Where have you chosen to live—the city, a rural environment, a small town? Who are the important people in your life? Are you in a committed relationship? How does this relationship nurture you as a woman? Who are your friends? How do they reflect your values? How does your relationship with your parents influence the choices you make?

What is your relationship to your body, your health, your sexuality? Are you active sexually and do you feel comfortable about expressing yourself as a sexual woman? What is your relationship to your emotions? Are you comfortable feeling and expressing your emotions? Are you comfortable listening to others?

How are you challenging your mind and what are you learning? What are your career goals, and how are you developing your creativity? How do you feel about being a woman at this time politically, spiritually, economically? What is your relationship to your community, and how do you want to play a part in it? What is your relationship to spirit, nature, your intuition? What part does spirituality play in your life? Become as aware as possible of yourself in your early twenties, remembering what was important to you and how the choices you made shaped you as a woman. Pause one minute or more. Now we will leave early adulthood and move to your early thirties.

Again, look down and notice your feet in your early thirties. What style and color shoes are you wearing, or are you barefoot? Become aware of your body in your early thirties—your legs, buttocks, pelvis, chest, breasts, back, shoulders, arms, hands, neck, face, and hair. How are you wearing your hair at this time? What color is it? What clothes are you wearing and how do your clothes and shoes reflect your role at this time in your life? What is your focus at this time in your life? Are you involved in your career, married, giving birth, raising children? How does being a mother affect how you feel about yourself as a woman? What is your relationship to your body and your health? What foods are important to you now? How do you manage your feelings?

Notice your environment. What are the colors, shapes, smells, tastes, and sounds in your environment? Where have you chosen to live—the city, a rural environment, a small town—and with whom? Who are the important people in your life? Who are your friends? What do they appreciate about you? Are you in a committed relationship, and how does that relationship challenge and nurture you?

What is your career? How are you managing your time? How do you set boundaries? How are you challenging yourself mentally and creatively? What are your goals and how are you actualizing them? How do you participate in your community, and what is your relationship to money?

What is your relationship to spirit? Do you have a relationship with divine spirit within yourself? How do the religious attitudes and beliefs with which you were raised affect your perception of yourself as a woman? What is your relationship to nature, your dreams, your intuition? Become as aware of yourself in your early thirties as possible. Let the images of your early thirties wash over you. Pause for a couple of minutes. Now, we will move on to your early forties.

Repeat the exercise as necessary for your forties, fifties, sixties, seventies, eighties (up to your present age), paying close attention to your awareness of your relationship to body, health, mind, creativity, emotions, and spirit, and how you have nurtured your dreams, strengths, and abilities.

Now, bring your attention to yourself at your present age. Still with your eyes closed, look down at your feet. What shoes are you wearing today? Become aware of your body—your legs, buttocks, pelvis, chest, breasts, back, shoulders, arms, hands, neck, face, and hair. How are you wearing your hair at this time? What color is it? What clothes are you wearing and how do your clothes reflect how you feel about yourself as a woman at present? How do you care for your health, strength, and stamina? How do you feel about your sexuality?

Become aware of the environment in which you have chosen to live and to work. Notice the colors, shapes, smells, tastes, and sounds in your environment. What is the music you listen to now? What do you eat? How are you nurtured by your environment?

What is the focus of your life at the present time—relationship, children, aging parents, career, artistic or academic goals, spiritual practice? Who are the important people in your life? What do they appreciate about you? What do you appreciate about yourself? What are you learning about your emotions and your mind? Are you comfortable expressing the full range of your emotions?

How are you challenging yourself and being challenged in your work? Do you feel competent and self-confident? How are you nurturing your creativity? What is your place in your community? What is your relationship to spirit, to nature, to your intuition, to your sense of yourself as a woman? What are your goals for the future?

Become aware of yourself at the present time. (Pause several minutes.) As you slowly bring yourself back to full waking consciousness, review the stages of your life, allowing the important images and memories to surface once again. In a moment, but not quite yet, count silently to ten. Open your eyes at ten, feeling relaxed and alert.

Draw, record, or write down all of the images that came to you during this exercise, whether or not you think they are important. Some of the images and feelings that emerged may be joyful; others may be surprising or painful. Give yourself permission to harvest all of the memories in detail, because you will find them helpful in working with other exercises throughout the book.

QUESTIONS FOR REFLECTION

* What have been the turning points or threshold experiences in your life? For example, a geographical move, parents' divorce, grandparent's death, childhood illness, incest, or accident, being accepted or rejected by a

certain group at school, learning to play an instrument, being banned from playing Little League softball because you're a girl, your first sexual experience, getting pregnant as a teenager, marriage, or giving birth.

* How did you respond to these turning points?
* In what way have you turned stressful experiences into positive growth experiences? Focus on your strength, creativity, and stamina as a result of any wounding.
* What did you learn about yourself and the people close to you?
* Are there any patterns that you have repeated at different stages of your life (victim of circumstances, martyr, peacemaker, seductress, drama queen, etc.)? Are these patterns satisfying or frustrating?

WRITING EXERCISE

Choose a threshold experience or turning point in your life and write about it in as much detail as possible. What was the road not taken?

DREAMS: GETTING STARTED

In working with your dreams, it is helpful to have a flashlight, dream journal with a pen, or a recorder next to your bed. Everyone dreams every night, but many people think they don't dream because they don't remember their dreams. Remembering a dream is a conscious practice, just like brushing your teeth. Writing it down or recording it helps facilitate the process.

The best time to catch a dream image is in the morning when you first wake up. Lie absolutely still and let the images from the night before rise to the surface of your consciousness. Don't move. I try to replay the dream images, somewhat like a movie, before I roll over. I find that once I move or reach for my dream journal, I frequently forget the dream. Once I have the dream image or narrative in my mind, I write it down. As I write, I often remember details of the dream I did not recall at first. I try to pay attention to the feelings in my body that the dream evokes or the memories that emerge.

How might your life have been different if there had been a place for you . . . a place of women, where you were received and affirmed? A place where other women, perhaps somewhat older, had been affirmed before you, each in her time, affirmed, as she struggled to become more truly herself. . . .

—JUDITH DUERK

A dream can be considered in two ways: what it reflects about your everyday life, and what it says about your inner life. Sometimes you will get a sense of what the dream means when you record it; at other times you have to work with the associations specific dream images provoke before you understand the dream's meaning. More will be said about working with dream associations in chapter 2.

Each night as you fall asleep, you may wish to prepare for dream recall by giving yourself the suggestion that you remember your dreams easily. Record each image you remember no matter how insignificant; it is a way to begin the process. Even a short, seemingly insignificant dream is trying to tell you something you need to know. Sometimes the "little" dreams have the most profound messages.

RECORD THE DREAMS YOU HAVE WHILE WORKING WITH THIS CHAPTER.

Separating from the Feminine and Identifying with the Masculine

There are many endings and many beginnings and there is always, between ending and beginning, the very briefest of moments and in those moments, change, deep volatile change, is possible. To find that moment, to grasp it, embrace it, to change within it, that is the thrust of evolution. That is the moment of chaos, of a higher order, the disorder of the gods, but order nevertheless.
—RHODA LERMAN, *The Book of the Night*

In a patriarchal society a woman splits from her feminine nature in her effort to be acceptable. The feminine, as represented by the mother, is demeaned, scapegoated, and stereotyped to the point that the archetypal image of Mother loses its soul as the individual mother is blamed for everyone's psychological deficits. The degree to which a woman's mother represents the status quo, the restrictive context of sexual roles and the deep-seated sense of female inferiority within a patriarchal society, determines the degree to which a woman will seek to separate herself from her mother. As she progresses through the stages of her development and begins to understand the roots of the devaluation of the feminine in this culture, she will realize that her mother is not the cause of her feelings of inadequacy. She is merely a convenient target to blame for the confusion and low self-esteem experienced by many women in a culture that glorifies the masculine.

The Heroine's Journey begins with the daughter's struggle to separate from the feminine, which is identified both physically and psychologically with her own mother and with the Mother archetype, which has an even greater hold. An archetype is an inborn pattern of images, ideas, and instinctual impulses that functions much like a hidden magnet; we cannot actually see such underlying patterns, but "we are propelled by their energy."[1] These archetypal images that come from the collective unconscious are the basic content of religions, mythologies, legends, and fairy tales.[2] The Mother archetype possesses extraordinary power and has an enormous influence on the psychic life of a child.[3] The woman who is the personal mother automatically inherits qualities and functions of mothers who have existed for hundreds of thousands of years; she carries the "pattern" of Mother. It is not essential that the woman who is the actual mother embody all of the attributes of the Mother archetype; indeed, none do. Yet the archetypal influence is so strong that when a young daughter looks at her mother, she sees not a mortal defined by age, personality, limited abilities, or social conditions, but a powerful figure who embodies the Good Mother or carries the shadow of the Devouring Mother, so popular in fairy tales.

> *The most conscientious way to honor one's father and mother is to "leave" them: to accept and understand, with gratitude, what has come through them and to take those motifs to their next level of expression.*
> —LINDA SUSSMAN

A daughter often separates from her feminine nature if she sees her mother carrying the negative pole of the archetype as emotionally controlling, rejecting, unavailable, or distant; angry, self-loathing, illogical; vulnerable, passive, manipulative, or powerless. Until very recently, many mothers were perceived in this way because women had so little choice about childbearing and child rearing and were denied entry into positions of authority. They had little power of their own and felt undervalued for the important job of mothering they assumed. Girls who wanted to develop a self-image separate from the family and compete in society had little choice but to reject the way of the mother and embrace the way of the father. Unfortunately, in an effort to do so, a girl may also reject many of her own positive feminine qualities of nurturing, relationship building, and emotional expressiveness to "get ahead."

The separation from the personal mother is a particularly intense process for a daughter because she has to separate from the one who is most like herself. She experiences a fear of loss characterized by anxiety about being alone, separate, and different from the one who in most cases has been her primary relationship. It is more complex for a daughter to separate from her mother than it is for a son because a daughter must differentiate herself from the one with whom she is supposed to identify, whereas the male child is taught to repudiate within himself his mother's qualities and behaviors in his efforts to become masculine.[4]

Many daughters experience a conflict between wanting a freer life than their mother's and wanting their mother's love and approval. They want to move beyond their mother yet fear risking the loss of their mother's love. Geographical separation may be the only way at first to resolve the tension between a daughter's need to grow up and her desire to please her mother.

Concurrent with her separation from her mother, a deep separation from the feminine occurs on a cultural level because of distorted images of the female body presented by the media and because of internalized messages that promote male prominence and domination in every echelon of society. If you ask an adolescent girl who has more power in her class, in the school, in the administration of her school, in the culture, she will say men. Although contemporary woman's position in society is more powerful than her mother's, she is still far from equal. And so, a young woman sets out to learn the strategies of competition and achievement that enable her to live up to male standards of performance. She begins to discredit her feelings, override her intuition, and ignore her body wisdom and dreams. And this happens long before she becomes a woman.

In *Reviving Ophelia,* the psychologist Mary Pipher writes, "Girls come of age in a misogynistic culture in which men have most political and economic power."[5] Most history books are written about the exploits of men. In adolescence, "girls are expected to sacrifice the parts of themselves that our culture considers masculine on the altar of social acceptability and to shrink their souls down to a petite size."[6] The "rules" for females have remained the same since the fifties: "Be attractive, be a lady, be unselfish and of service, make relationships work and be competent without complaint."[7]

We all know young girls who are full of life and vitality at eight, nine, and ten, tomboys who love to climb trees, express their opinions, explore the natural world, and share their optimism. These same girls become mere shadows of their former selves as they enter adolescence. They deny their true gifts and their true nature as they adopt false selves to please the adult culture. The part of them they deem unacceptable goes underground and eventually withers from lack of attention or gets projected onto someone else.

Pipher writes, "Girls become 'female impersonators' who fit their whole selves into small, crowded spaces. Vibrant, confident girls become shy, doubting young women. Girls stop thinking, 'Who am I / What do I want?' and start thinking, 'What must I do to please others?'"[8] The young female learns to please, perform, and placate. She also learns to devalue her female body. Every time she turns on the television she sees women sexualized and objectified, their bodies marketed to sell cars and toothpaste. There is such contempt for the female body that it is difficult for a young girl to feel comfortable and proud of her own. As a result she tries to conform to cultural images of the ideal female and begins to lose confidence in herself.

In classes, boys are twice as likely to be seen as role models, five times as likely to receive teachers' attention and twelve times as likely to speak up in class.
—MARY PIPHER

If a girl feels alienated from who she is as a young woman, it makes sense that she will search for recognition from the masculine-dominated culture. Individuals in a patriarchal culture are driven to seek control over themselves and others in an inhuman desire for perfection. Women seek power and authority either by becoming like men or by becoming liked by men. This is not such a negative thing at first, because seeking male validation is a healthy transition from fusion with the mother to greater independence in society. The young woman who identifies with what could be considered positive father qualities, such as discipline, decision making, direction, protection, power, and self-valuation, finds herself achieving success in the world. This can be very damaging, however, if a woman believes that she does not exist except in the mirror of male attention and definition.

Approval and encouragement by her father or other father figures usually lead to a woman's positive ego development, but lack of genuine involvement or negative involvement on the part of the father, stepfather, brother, uncle, or grandfather deeply wounds a woman's sense of herself. It can lead to overcompensation and perfectionism or virtually paralyze her development. Many women try to identify with their father's sense of power and visibility but have not been taught the skills to achieve their own goals. When a father is absent or indifferent to his daughter, he indicates his disinterest, disappointment, and disapproval, which can be as damaging as explicit negative judgments or overprotection.

FATHERS' DAUGHTERS

A father's daughter is a woman who usually had a close positive (or highly conflicted) relationship with her father as a child and maintains a close connection to him as an adult. She identifies with her father and idealizes him and therefore identifies primarily with males and masculine values, often seeing women and female values and opinions as secondary. Central to being a father's daughter is the rejection of or by the mother; she becomes the weak link in the triangle. Nowhere is this primal triangle more vividly depicted than in the ancient myth of the goddess Athena, patroness of Athens and Greek civilization. Athena is the archetype of the father's daughter in that she is allied with her father in the rejection of her mother.

The myth begins with Athena's birth, in which she springs full grown from her *father's* head, wearing flashing gold armor, holding a sharp spear in one hand, and emitting a mighty war cry. Her father, Zeus, actually *stole* Athena from her mother, Metis, while Metis was pregnant. Because Zeus feared that Metis would bear a child equal to him in courage and wise counsel, he thwarted fate by tricking his consort into becoming small and swallowing her. With this act, he took away her ability to give birth and stole their daughter for himself. Following this dramatic birth, Athena associated herself only with Zeus, acknowledging him as her sole parent. Though less mythic in stature, this is what also happens to a father's daughter: the mother is metaphorically swallowed by the father as he steals the daughter for himself.[9]

> *Girls are exposed to almost three times as many boy-centered stories as girl-centered stories. Because with boys failure is attributed to external factors and success is attributed to ability, they keep their confidence, even with failure. With girls it's just the opposite. Because their success is attributed to good luck or hard work and failure to lack of ability, with every failure, a girl's confidence is eroded.*
>
> —MARY PIPHER

If the young heroine has rejected her mother, or has been rejected by her, she views her personal father as heroic; he has freedom and the privilege to come and go as he pleases. He has power and status. She wants to be like her father, to be liked by her father, sometimes even to be her father. She strives not only to know her father's innermost thoughts and feelings but also to experience the type of power and visibility he holds in the world.[10]

In adolescence, her relationship with her father may become overintellec-tualized; they engage in dialogue, debate, and the exchange of ideas, thereby elevating her mind and undermining her emerging sexuality. One woman I in-terviewed for *Fathers' Daughters* talked about this phenomenon as the "erotic brain." She said the message she got from her father was that it was imperative to have a fine mind and to use it to succeed in the world. The whole arena of love and sexuality was never discussed. As a result, she neutralized her sexuality and became a very successful editor in the publishing industry. Yet, still single in her early forties, she yearns to have a loving relationship.

In such an identification with the masculine, the young woman lives out her father's projected image of her, and it takes her a long time to discover her identity separate from his. Many women in this situation also have difficulty reconciling achievement and relationship, which they see as incompatible. They therefore have trouble maintaining close intimate relations.

The young heroine begins to see men and the male world as adult and be-comes identified with the internal masculine voice that tells her that her value is determined by her achievement, production, and success. She has high expectations of herself and others, little empathy for limits, and won't allow herself to get sick. She seeks to emulate her father at all costs. Adoring him, she internalizes his values and dictates as the inner voice that drives her, demanding that she be productive.

> My role as a feminist is not to compete with men in their world—that's too easy, and ultimately unproductive. My job is to live fully as a woman, enjoying the whole of myself and my place in the universe.
> —MADELEINE L'ENGLE

As a consequence, a father's daughter is ambitious and responsible in the world of work; she has the focus and deter-mination to achieve her goals and often accepts responsibility for more than she can comfortably handle. She demands per-fection from herself and has little tolerance for her own vul-nerability. In an effort not to be like a woman, she becomes like a man, thinks like a man, and works harder than a man. She is considered a success by the standards of a patriarchal, goal-oriented, power-based culture. In the work world she may emulate a masculine work style, or she may become so-licitous of, play mother to, or become the confidante of a man in power. Even if she does not enter the work world, her inner voice is masculine and perfection-istic and she projects her ambitions and need for achievement on her children, weary from enrichment classes and sports scheduled every day after school.

QUESTIONS FOR WRITING AND REFLECTION: YOU AND YOUR MOTHER

If your mother was absent, you may wish to answer these questions in relationship to a family friend or female relative who served as a mother figure.

* How did you feel about yourself as a female child?
* What was your relationship with your mother?
* How did your mother feel about being a woman?
* What did she teach you about being a woman?
* Did you admire your mother? How did she inspire you?
* What are her values that you embody?
* What did your mother teach you about your body?
* How did she respond to your first menstruation?
* What did she teach you about your sexuality?
* What are you teaching (or did you teach) your daughter about her body and her sexuality?
* How were you conditioned to be a good girl?
* What parts of yourself were allowed expression when you were a girl?
* What parts of yourself were not allowed expression when you were a girl?
* What were your activities, ambitions, and dreams when you were nine?
* When did you first encounter the limitations of being a girl (physically, creatively, intellectually)? Were you encouraged to go beyond limitations?
* Do you have a memory of splitting off from being female (in your body, emotionally, denying dreams and goals)? When?
* What decision did you make about yourself as a girl?
* Who are the women in your womanline (family members), and what early memories do you have of them?
* How were you influenced by female characters in the media or in literature?
* How were you influenced by female athletes, artists, politicians, public figures?
* Did you have female mentors or models (grandmother, aunt, friend, teacher) who inspired you with the way they lived their lives?
* What images of the feminine do you carry in your dreams?

* What were the cultural myths about being a woman when you were growing up?

WRITING EXERCISES

* Write in detail about an experience you had as a young girl or adolescent that illustrates your comfort or discomfort with being female. Was there ever a time that you didn't want to be female? Why? (For instance, maybe your brother had more freedom and privileges than you and you wanted to be like him.)
* Write or record a story about your relationship with your mother. How did she encourage you? How did she hold you back? What aspect of your mother do you still carry?

QUESTIONS FOR WRITING AND REFLECTION: YOU AND YOUR FATHER

If your father was absent, you may wish to answer these questions in relationship to a family friend or male relative who served as a father figure.

* What was your relationship with your father like?
* What is your earliest memory of your father?
* How did he spend time with you?
* What games did he play with you?
* What did he call you?
* In what ways did you identify with him?
* What did he value?
* How did you try to please him?
* What did he expect of you?
* Did he treat you like a son?
* Did he listen to your feelings?
* Did he listen to and respect your opinions? Which ones?
* What guidance did he give you?

* Were you his confidante?
* How did he treat your emerging sexuality?
* What message did he give you about being a woman?
* What is your strongest image of him?
* What was his weakness?
* How did he show his love?
* What is the greatest gift of himself that he gave to you?
* What does the voice of your father say inside your head?
* What are the masculine images in your dreams?

> *Many of us are unaware of our devotion to the values and standards which our "fathers" represent. We have unconsciously accepted ourselves as daughters, and unconsciously act out little girl roles in relation to men.*
> —MARION WOODMAN,
> "The Emergence of the Feminine," in *Betwixt and Between*

WRITING EXERCISES

* One of the ways a girl splits off from her feminine nature is to deny, avoid, or repress her feelings. What decisions did you make about how to manage your emotions as a result of your father's response to your feelings?

When my father was playful, I felt _____

         happy _____

         proud _____

         attentive _____

         angry _____

         sad _____

         frustrated _____

         disappointed _____

         distant _____

         rejecting _____

         uncertain _____

When I felt angry, my father was _____

         sad _____

         frustrated _____

disappointed	_____
distant	_____
uncertain	_____
happy	_____
loving	_____

* Write or record a memory illustrating your relationship with your father, including the messages he gave you about being female.

DREAM PERSONALITIES

Dreams show you, in symbolic form, all the different personalities that interact within you and make up your total self. Each person in a dream is an aspect of yourself. Even if a dream seems to be about someone else, it is usually telling you something that you don't know or don't recognize about yourself.

For example, if you dream about your mother or father, the dream is most likely using the image of your parent to represent a quality in you, a conflict within you, or something evolving in you that has little to do with your physical parent. Sometimes we take the dream image literally, particularly if we are in conflict with the person who appears in the dream. You have to remember that you have an inner mother or father who is part of you that you need to take seriously. You need to stop blaming your personal parent for any conflicts you have with your inner parent, because these are conflicts within yourself. Try to understand what part of you your parent represents and what he or she is trying to communicate to you.[11]

RECORD THE DREAMS YOU HAVE WHILE WORKING WITH THIS CHAPTER.

The Road of Trials

The transformative act for a woman, then, can be seeking her own good and advancement and facing her terror of being alone. The transformative act for a man is often putting aside his terror of being swallowed up by feminine connectedness and risking genuine intimacy.
—CAROL S. PEARSON, *Awakening the Heroes Within*

The heroine crosses the threshold, leaves her parents' home, and goes in search of her self. In all heroic quests there is a call: when a woman has outgrown her old reality, something enters in to invite her to move beyond the safety of the known self. It is a call to growth, and it can bring profound suffering. She is challenged to create herself anew and to undertake the challenge no matter how frightened she may feel. The fear and feelings of inadequacy that surface when one responds to a call is the reason that many of us spend years successfully ignoring the urge for growth.

After crossing the threshold, the heroine gathers allies, confronts adversaries, and begins her road of trials. In early adulthood, this outer road of trials will take her through the developmental tasks of adulthood in our culture. Achieving goals such as academic degrees, prestigious titles, corporate promotions, artistic acclaim, finding loving relationships, and establishing financial stability are all part of a woman's search for identity. The actualization of these goals in the outer world and the personal growth that occurs through the process of achieving them are the boon of success. As she works through these outer tests, the heroine will also encounter the forces of her own self-doubt, self-hate, indecisiveness, paralysis, and fear. The outer world might tell her she can do it, but

she battles with demons and adversaries who tell her she can't.

The first adversary will reassure her that it's all right to Play It Safe: "Why do you want to venture out anyway? It's so comfortable here." This inner adversarial voice will implore her to cling to the past: old patterns of behavior, old relationships, an old lifestyle. The heroine must move forward even when she wants to retreat. She must believe in herself and the integrity of her quest even when she feels nothing but doubt. Her allies will be hope and perseverance even when she is experiencing only emptiness and pain. Her resistance and fear will have to be overcome by a fierce act of indomitable will.[1]

The second adversary is the Myth of Dependency. Women have been encouraged to be dependent, to give up their needs for another's love, and to take care of the dependency needs of others. Yet at the same time, because of the archetypal covenant made between fathers (parents) and daughters, most women unconsciously believe that someone else will provide for them. Even if they grow up believing themselves to be equal in intelligence and talent to men, there is an ingrained belief that someone else will ultimately take care of them. Many women are actually socialized to appear less intelligent, less competent, and less successful than they are and to interrupt their careers when demands of partners or children interfere. They may also be taught that their career and financial success will undermine their partner's self-esteem as provider for the family.

If I didn't start painting, I would have raised chickens.
—GRANDMA MOSES

Another adversary the heroine will meet on her journey is the Myth of Female Inferiority or deficit thinking. We live in an androcentric society, which sees the world from a male point of view. In many families, cultures, and religions, female children are considered inferior to males; being born in a female body is second rate. In such cases, girls have failed from the start and are always playing catch-up to the all-powerful, highly regarded boy child. This prejudice pervades language and opinions as well. The mother tongue, the language of experience, is given less validation than the father tongue, the language of analysis. And whether we are consciously aware of it or not, a litany of deficit thinking pervades our inner voice as well.

Each of us has an inner voice that serves as a critic. In women, this inner critic is particularly strong. You may have noticed that women tend to be critical of *themselves,* whereas, in general, men tend to judge *others.* Most women have an inner critic known as the Inner Patriarch, which values traditionally masculine-oriented ideas and opinions and devalues anything traditionally considered feminine. This Inner Patriarch mirrors the outer societal beliefs about the inferiority of women and carries the weight of at least five thousand years of patriarchal thinking. This is one of the reasons that women have a much stronger inner critic than men do and have to fight harder to separate from its beliefs.[2] They struggle not only with the voice of the culture that devalues women but, more important, with their own inner mantra extolling their deficits.

The best thing you can do with your Inner Critic is to identify the sound of its voice, give it a name, and send it on vacation. I always suggest to my writing students to leave the critic outside the door when they are about to sit down to write or read their work. The Inner Critic has dampened more creative projects than all of our naysayers combined! If you have a particularly tenacious Inner Critic who refuses to be silenced, notice if there is a positive function it could serve, and employ it for that task only. For example, if your Inner Critic berates you constantly for procrastinating, ask it to help you to schedule a time to begin a particular project. The Inner Critic will disrupt your peace less if it has a job to do.

The heroine must also confront the Myth of Romantic Love, which says that a woman must search for a partner, male or female—who will solve her problems and fill the hole of her yearning. This figure will rescue her. Women are trained into a state of expectancy and have lived too long with a desire for closure by another—"If he or she notices me . . . ," "If I marry him or her . . . ,"

> *Within most women is an Inner Patriarch who believes that she is indeed inferior and that she needs constant surveillance to keep her behavior appropriate! It feels a deep-seated disdain for her femaleness and can literally make her ashamed to be a woman.*
> —HAL STONE & SIDRA STONE

"If I get that job . . . ," When we move . . . ," and so on. Unconsciously, a woman hopes that once something is settled in the external world, she will be content. This sets up a state of passivity for a woman, as she waits for something or someone else to actualize her destiny. A transformation occurs not as the result of a rescue from without but from enormous growth and development within a woman's psyche over a long period of time. A woman must abandon the hope for rescue and closure so that her own adventures can begin.[3] Only then does she grow out of a "daughter" psychology.

> A major task for many women becomes how to enlist men's involvement for more intimacy on their part, and how to have less self-sacrifice on our part so that we don't wear out our good will.
> —KAREN SIGNELL

Women must also confront the Myth of Never Being Enough: No matter how many outer goals a woman has accomplished, she never feels that she has done enough. In the quest for success in an acquisitive society, achievement becomes an addiction. The focus is on performance, striving, and pushing limits. Women, in general, have a difficult time feeling a sense of triumph and sustaining a sense of satisfaction. We are always seeking more validation, and we succumb to the expectations and demands of others. The single greatest challenge for most women is to achieve balance among relationships, work, and time alone. *Women have to be willing to find the courage to set limits and say no.* We also have to be willing to be limited and accept the fact that there are many things we can do nothing about.

I was surprised to find myself grappling with the Myth of Never Being Enough as a newly separated single woman when my husband of eleven years and I divorced. Although I considered myself to be successful in my career and as a mother raising my children, I felt like a failure. We are such a coupled society that being single—for whatever reason—makes one feel like an amputee. Some women who choose not to bear children suffer from this same myth in not fulfilling the biological expectation inherent in being female.

PSYCHE AND EROS

Many myths and fairy tales illustrate the ways in which a psyche develops and survives. Some fairy tales describe the "healthy" development of an individual psyche. The tale of Psyche and Eros illustrates some of the trials a woman endures as she separates from the collective while maintaining a relationship to the divine.

Psyche is the youngest of three daughters and so beautiful that people start to compare her to the goddess of femininity, Aphrodite. Psyche is the distress of her parents because, although her two older sisters are happily married, no one asks for her hand. Her father, a king, goes to an oracle dominated by Aphrodite, who, jealous of Psyche, declares that she is to be taken to the top of a mountain, chained there, and married to a horrible creature.

Aphrodite instructs her son, Eros, the god of love, to inflame Psyche with love for the horrible creature who will come to claim her at midnight, but when Eros sees Psyche, he accidentally pricks his finger on one of his own arrows and falls in love with her. He decides to take Psyche for his own bride and lifts her down from the mountain to the Valley of Paradise. Psyche awakens to find that she is married to this magnificent god-husband who is with her every night and puts only one restriction on her. He makes her promise that she will not look at him and will not ask him his business. She may have anything she wishes but she must question nothing. Psyche agrees to this and lives happily for a while, unquestioning, until her two sisters try to visit.

At first Eros warns Psyche that her inquisitive sisters will bring disaster, but he eventually relents, and the sisters visit. The sisters want to know everything about Psyche's husband, and she makes up several stories until they realize that she does not know him. They suggest that Eros is really a loathsome creature who will eat her child when the baby is born. They advise Psyche to get a covered lamp and a knife and to kill her husband as he sleeps. That night, as Eros sleeps, Psyche takes the cover off the lamp, grasps the knife, and looks at him. In that moment she sees that he is the god of love, drops the knife, and accidentally pricks herself with one of Eros's arrows. She immediately falls in love with him. At the same time, a drop of oil from the lamp falls on Eros's shoulder, and he awakens and flies away with Psyche clinging to him. Tiring, she falls to earth, and Eros leaves her.

In her despair at Eros's flight, Psyche immediately wants to drown herself in a river. Pan is at the river and dissuades Psyche from taking her life. He tells her that she must pray to the goddess of love, who understands when someone is inflamed with love. Psyche realizes that she must go to Aphrodite herself, who reluctantly gives her four tasks as a condition for her deliverance.

First, Aphrodite shows Psyche a huge pile of seeds of many different kinds mixed together and tells her she must sort them before nightfall or die.

Psyche waits, ants hear of her dilemma, and they sort the seeds into different mounds for her.

The second task Aphrodite begrudgingly gives Psyche is to go into a certain field across a river and bring back fleece from the golden rams of the sun before nightfall. Once more, faced with this daunting task, Psyche thinks of throwing herself into the river, but the reeds at the water's edge speak to her and tell her not to approach the rams during the day but to go at dusk and take some of the rams' wool that has been caught on the low-hanging branches of the trees. She will find enough to satisfy Aphrodite.

In the third task, Aphrodite instructs Psyche to fill a crystal goblet with water from the river Styx, which is guarded by dangerous monsters. When Psyche feels defeated, an eagle of Zeus appears, flies to the center of the stream, lowers the goblet into the dangerous waters, fills it, and returns it to Psyche.

The fourth task is the most interesting. Psyche must go into the underworld and obtain a box of beauty ointment from Persephone herself. Psyche thinks this is impossible and again feels defeated. This time a tower gives her instructions. She is to take two coins in her mouth and two pieces of barley bread. She must refuse to assist a lame donkey driver who will ask her to pick up some sticks, pay the ferryman over the river Styx with one of the coins, refuse the groping hand of a dying man who reaches up out of the water, refuse to assist three women who are weaving the threads of fate. She is to throw one piece of barley bread to Cerberus, the three-headed dog who guards the entrance to the underworld, and go in while the heads are quarreling over the bread. She must then repeat the process in reverse. Psyche gets the beauty ointment and brings it back to the upper world past all the trials and temptations, only to open the box when she returns. A deadly sleep immediately falls over her and she falls to the ground as if dead.

At this point Eros appears, wipes the sleep off her, puts it back into the box, and takes Psyche up with him to Olympus. There he talks with Zeus, who agrees that Psyche has satisfactorily completed all the tasks and shall be made a goddess. Aphrodite concurs. The gods agree and Eros and Psyche are married, and Psyche gives birth to a girl, whom they name Pleasure.[4]

Psyche is a woman who has yet to move out of a daughter psychology. She has known nothing except her parents' home, and when she is transported into the Valley of Paradise by Eros to be his bride, she accepts her fate and asks no questions. She is relieved to be rescued from the jaws of the horrible creature and is willing to remain unconscious of the person to whom she is married. This is what happens to most of us when we first marry; we are willing to remain in a state of illusion until something forces us to shine the light of illumination on ourselves and our relationship. Psyche was forced into consciousness by her sisters' insistence that she find out more about her husband. She shines the light of illumination on him, falls in love with what she *sees,* and loses him immediately.

She is abandoned, paradise is over, and she must face life on her own. Her loss sends her to the river, where she wants to drown her sorrows. But she is persuaded by Pan not to take the easy way out and to begin her own journey of individuation. She must go to the goddess of love herself and be tested.

The tasks given to her by Aphrodite represent some of the tests the feminine psyche must struggle with in order to grow. First, Psyche must sort seeds. As you know, every element of a dream or a fairy tale is an aspect of the self. So the ants that come to help her are that part of her psyche that must sort out possibilities, make order out of confusion, and learn to rely on her own psychological, intellectual, and intuitive tools to make sense of what she faces alone. A woman must fine-tune the sword of discrimination to decide what serves her life and what must be cut away.

In the second task, Psyche must find her own feminine power. She must acquire some fleece from aggressive rams whose primary task is to assert domination. She must listen to her own instinctual voice and cultivate patience so that she does not act too quickly and bring about her own destruction. She has to find a way of getting a symbol of power for herself without being destroyed in the process. This is the test many women face every day in a patriarchal culture. Challenged to overcome the Myth of Female Inferiority, they must attain the power they seek without armoring themselves and disconnecting from their feelings and feminine soul.

The third task symbolizes Psyche's need to develop an overview of a situation so that she doesn't collapse into fear. The perspective of the eagle enables her to see the patterns of her life so that she doesn't fall into repetitive self-sabotaging behavior in relationships or in work.

The fourth task is the hardest for almost every woman because she must impose limits on herself and others and admit to herself that it is acceptable to be limited. Psyche accomplishes the fourth task by saying no to those who want

It is easier to fight an enemy outside than an enemy within. It is important for women to know that an Inner Patriarch exists within them, that patriarchy is not just an enemy to be battled on the outside.
—HAL STONE & SIDRA STONE

her help. For each of us to refrain from abdicating ourselves, we must stop rescuing others and acknowledge that everyone has their own destiny. Only then can we become whole ourselves.

As Psyche returns from the underworld she cannot contain her curiosity and opens the casket of Persephone's beauty ointment. She falls into a deadly sleep, becoming unconscious. This failure reminds her that she is human and reminds us that we will always meet failure along our path. We make mistakes, we betray ourselves, we slide backward. But we also learn from each misstep. This is part of being human. We cannot expect perfection, and each time we fall, another part of our psyche, like Eros in the myth, will raise us to consciousness.

ALLIES

The ally is a figure frequently found in dreams, myths, and stories who aids or protects the heroine. In the story of Psyche and Eros, Psyche has assistance from various allies: ants help her sort the seeds, reeds tell her how to gather the golden fleece, an eagle fills the crystal goblet, and a tower gives her instructions for her underworld journey. Eros wipes a deadly sleep off Psyche and takes her to Olympus to be made a goddess. When Psyche loses faith and wants to drown herself in the river, Pan is the ally who encourages her to go on.

An ally has usually survived his or her own trials and can now pass on her knowledge and wisdom to another. The ally guides us on the road of life and motivates us to stay with our journey no matter how difficult it is to overcome our fears. Some allies help us cross the threshold; others assist us when we are tested, are fair witness to what is going on in our lives, and give us perspective about our journeys. An ally often asks a clarifying question about our journey, such as "Where are you going and how are you going to get there?"

We develop a relationship with our inner ally as we develop more awareness of the Self. The Self is the wiser, more goddesslike part of ourselves.[5] Our inner ally often embodies qualities of the people who have assisted us at different times throughout our lives. To become more aware of your inner ally, recall the people who have appeared at different points in your life to support, guide, nurture, and inspire you.

ADVERSARIES

Just as there are allies in our lives and ally parts of our nature, there are also adversaries or threshold guardians whose function it is to test or block our progress. Adversaries challenge us by saying: "Are you really serious about wanting to make this change? Do you think you can do it? Don't you think your children will suffer? What about your partner? Isn't it an economic risk?" The adversary stands for our internal demons: the emotional scars, dependencies, resistances, and self-limitations that hold back our growth. Every time we try to change an old pattern or move forward, an adversary surfaces to test whether or not we are serious.

We have already looked at how the myths of female inferiority, dependency, and romantic love serve as adversaries and are deeply embedded in our culture. The following story of Bluebeard, from Clarissa Pinkola Estes's *Women Who Run with the Wolves,* illustrates the adversary acting as a saboteur in a young woman's life.[6]

There was a man named Bluebeard who courted three sisters at the same time. At first they were afraid of him because of the cast of his beard, but in time the youngest daughter was charmed by him and agreed to marry him. Bluebeard and his new wife rode off to his castle in the woods. One day Bluebeard came to his new bride and told her he had to take a journey. He suggested that she invite her sisters to keep her company while he was away and gave her his ring of keys so that she would have access to all the rooms in the castle, except one. He forbade her to use the smallest key.

Bluebeard rode off and the sisters came to visit. When the young bride told them they had access to every room in the castle, they had a great time opening each door, finding out what lay behind it. They eventually came to the cellar, and the only key they had not used was the smallest, forbidden key. They were intrigued by a small door in the cellar, and the sisters implored the young bride to use the forbidden key to open the door. At first she was reluctant to disobey her husband, but then she opened the door. It was too dark to see inside, so the sisters brought a lamp to illumine the space, and when all three sisters looked within, they screamed. For the room was filled with bones of corpses thrown helter-skelter

> *When you travel with your enemies as your companions, when you offer them hands well-worn with compassion, when you shelter them in your wonder, then who you are and who you might be converge. You experience a sense of responsibility for the world around you—not because you are good, but because you are able to love.*
>
> —DAWNA MARKOVA

all around and with skulls stacked in corners. Shaking with terror, they slammed the door, grabbed the key out of the lock, and then looked down at the key. It was stained with blood. Everything the young wife did to remove the blood from the key proved useless. She just couldn't staunch the flow. She scoured the key with horsehair, pressed ashes onto it, and held it to the heat to sear it. She laid cobwebs over it, but nothing would stop the flow of blood. Finally she gave up and hid the key in her closet, where the key continued to bleed on her magnificent clothes.

The next day her husband returned and asked how everything had gone in his absence. She replied that everything was fine, and Bluebeard asked her to return his keys. When she gave him the key ring, he immediately saw that the smallest key was missing.

The young bride made excuses about losing the key while out riding, but Bluebeard did not believe her. He threw open her closet and saw that the smallest key had bled all over her gowns.

In a rage, Bluebeard grabbed his wife and roared that it was now her turn to die. He dragged her down into the cellar to the little room and immediately the door opened before him. There lay the skeletons of all of his previous wives.

The young wife pleaded for her life and asked to be given time to prepare for her death. Bluebeard relented, telling her she had a quarter hour to prepare herself, and she raced up to her room calling to her sisters. "Sisters, sisters, do you see our brothers coming?" At first they said no, and she kept repeating her plea. As Bluebeard began to come up the stairs after her, the brothers finally appeared. Thundering on horseback down the castle hallway, they chased Bluebeard out onto the parapet. There they killed him and left him to rot.

This story is similar to that of Psyche because again there are three sisters and the youngest is the most naïve. In the story of Bluebeard the youngest sister has not yet perceived her inner adversary or predator and sees only what she wants to see. Most of us contain a part of our psyche that refuses to see any aspect of our own destructive or self-defeating nature. Until her sisters encourage her to look behind every door, the young bride remains unconscious of the dangers with which she lives. She is forbidden to use the one key that could bring her to consciousness.

It is important for her to disobey the adversary's order and to find out what is behind the door. It is hard to look, but to become conscious, each one of us must look at the parts of ourselves that we deny or that have been killed or lie dying. The young sister wants to look away, but she cannot deny what she sees because the little key that opens the door keeps bleeding, and there is no way that she can hide the flow of blood. There has been a deep wound to the very core of her being.

When her husband returns, he knows immediately that she has found the carnage. He is prepared to kill her on the spot, but she asks to prepare herself. She needs time to center and strengthen herself to overwhelm her inner predator. She calls upon her brothers, her own inner masculine nature, for help in dismembering the adversary. Instead of collapsing helplessly, denying, or running away, she confronts the adversary head-on, eliminating the hold he has on her.

Every woman has an inner adversary, predator, or saboteur that keeps her from listening to her own intuition and following her truth. A woman must face this inner adversary and overcome it if she is to continue on her journey. Our inner adversary or saboteur often embodies aspects of people we have known throughout our lives who have made life difficult for us or thwarted our progress. Or they may embody shadow aspects of ourselves, those parts of ourselves that we don't want to see, such as neediness, blame, rigidity, aggressiveness, unrealistic expectations, perfectionism, intolerance, and self-pity.

ALLY EXERCISE

How have your parents, grandparents, teachers, coaches, priests, rabbis, lovers, children, friends, work associates served as allies for you? What did they value about you? How did they define you? How did you define yourself in their presence? How did they encourage you? Have any of the people with whom you have had difficult relationships functioned as allies by challenging you to stretch, grow, and confront parts of yourself you do not wish to look at? What have been the gifts (skills, attitudes, wisdom, insight) your allies have given you?

In what ways are you similar to the allies in your life? How do your strengths, skills, and attitudes remind you of them?

Make a list like the one below of all of the allies you have had in your life from early childhood to the present. How did they guide or assist you? What did they teach you about yourself? Include on your list your own ally characteristics. What parts of yourself can you count on? What part of you is your greatest ally?

ALLY	GIFT	ALLY PARTS OF MYSELF
Heather	positive outlook	looking for the light in the dark
Margaret	humor	ability to laugh at myself
Fernando	centeredness	desire to stay present
Nora	compassion	ability to listen deeply

ADVERSARY EXERCISE

As you did with your allies, make a list like the one below of all of the adversaries/enemies you have had in your life from early childhood to the present. You may discover that the same people can function as both allies and adversaries. How did they negate you or sabotage you? What behaviors did you develop to overcome their challenges? Include on your list the adversarial aspects of your own nature. How do you overcome them? What part of yourself has been your greatest adversary?

ADVERSARY	QUALITY	ADVERSARIAL PART OF MY NATURE
Mom	negativity	sees glass as half empty
Dad	left me unprotected	weak inner protector
Lucien	rejecting	self-negating

GUIDED IMAGERY: THE ALLY

Close your eyes and focus your attention on your breath moving in . . . and . . . out of your nostrils. Take three deep breaths, and as you exhale release any tension you may be carrying in any part of your body. As you breathe at your own rate, give yourself the suggestion that with each exhalation you move deeper and deeper into levels of consciousness where more images and memories are accessible to you. Now imagine that you are on a path in a forest. As you walk along the path, you notice the trees around you, the thick underbrush, and the sound of the birds. You notice the colors and smells. You feel the warmth of the sun and a gentle breeze. You continue along the path until you hear the sound of water. You see a small river before you, and you walk to the water's edge. As you look into the water, you are aware of your own reflection. You look at the stones and boulders in the water and think about your life. (Pause briefly.)

As you watch your own reflection in the water, you become aware of another presence standing next to you. You feel completely safe, as if this other presence was someone you have known for a very long time. This presence may be that of an old, wise woman or man, an animal, a friend who is your ally, someone you can trust. You greet each other, and your ally beckons to you to follow across a small bridge that crosses the river. You follow and find yourself climbing a hill that leads to a cave. Your ally enters the cave, sits down, and gestures for you to follow. You enter the cave and sit down, and your ally asks you how you are now being challenged in your life. The ally listens and then gives you a gift. This gift may be a wisdom story, a symbol of something that you need for your journey, words of reassurance, a task to complete. (Pause for one minute.)

You accept the gift, and the ally tells you that you may return at any time you wish. You are always welcome, and your ally will always be there to help you with anything you need. You thank your ally, take your gift with you, and leave the cave. You walk back down the path over the bridge, looking once again at your reflection in the water. You notice how you feel as you walk up the path, out of the forest, and then you bring yourself back here to full waking consciousness. Count to three to yourself and slowly open your eyes, feeling relaxed and alert.

WRITING EXERCISE: THE ALLY

Write or record your experience with your ally in this exercise and what he or she has taught you about yourself. What is the gift you have received? What does it mean to you? Is there a task that you have been instructed to complete?

QUESTIONS FOR WRITING AND REFLECTION

* What are the ways in which your Inner Critic (or Inner Patriarch) serenades you with your deficits? For example, "You'll never make

enough money," "You don't know enough to run that meeting," "You're too old to change careers."

* What does your Inner Critic say about your body, your appearance, your mind, your ability to have a successful relationship, and so forth? For example, "Your thighs are too heavy," "You'll never find another mate," "You just don't know how to dress," etc.
* Visualize your Inner Critic as clearly as you can. What does she or he look like? How does she dress? What is the sound of her voice? Who does she remind you of? Give her a name so that you'll recognize her in the future. Draw a picture of her. Send her on vacation.
* What are your personal myths about romantic love?
* What is the gift of yourself that you bring to your family, friends, community, work, yourself?
* What gift was given to you that has had an impact on your life? How? (For example, Patricia's grandfather gave her a gold coin when she was a young girl. She is now a very successful businesswoman who owns and runs a progressive bookstore.)

BRAG SHEET

Review and acknowledge your strengths, skills, talents. Who have you been as a woman? What have been your roles and accomplishments throughout your life? Write a brag sheet in the first person: for example, "I have been a wife, mother of two, manager of a restaurant," and so on.

A man must think about feelings before he talks about them, while a woman can feel, talk, and think all at the same time.
—JOHN GRAY

Use 12" x 18" paper or larger and write as quickly as you can using colored markers. If you wish, write it as a plaid with your present life superimposed on your early life.

Then write a one-to-two-page story about this character (yourself) in the third person. Depict the character (which can be either a person or an animal) embodying all of your qualities and strengths. For example, "Once upon a time there was a wee small girl who grew to be a wise and valiant warrior who . . ." or "Once upon a time there was a sleek black panther with a keen sense of smell who . . ." Share your story with a partner or speak or sing it into a recorder.

WRITING EXERCISE: THE ADVERSARY

Write or record a story about an experience you have had with an adversary from the *adversary's* point of view. Not your point of view—you already know that. Instead, tell the story from the adversary's perspective about what happened between you.

In looking at your adversary from this perspective, what did you learn? For example, at one time I had a particularly negative and depressive boss. I wrote a story about an interaction we had from her point of view, and I developed new compassion for her and what was going on in her life. I also had to acknowledge my own intolerance and arrogance in dealing with her.

DREAM ASSOCIATIONS

Most people who work with their dreams make associations to the images in them. After you record your dream, take the first image that grabs your attention, write it down, and ask yourself, "What feeling do I have about this image: what words or ideas come to mind as I look at it?"[7] Write down any word, feeling, or memory that the image evokes. Your associations may or may not have anything to do with what is going on in your waking life. Write down all the associations you find for that image; always go back to the original dream image to make your association rather than making connections with the association. Then go on to the next image.

As you read your associations, one will generate a lot of energy because it touches a wound, helps you see something in yourself that you have overlooked, or fits together with the other symbols in the dream. Go to the association that generates the most energy.[8]

After you have made associations to the images you have chosen, you need to figure out what is going on inside yourself that is represented by the situation in the dream. Robert Johnson suggests that you go back to each image and ask:

* What part of me is that?
* What qualities does this dream character have in real life?
* Do I have any traits in common with the person in the dream?

* Have I been acting out these traits lately in my waking life?
* Who is it, inside me, who feels like this or behaves like this?
* What beliefs or opinions does this character have?
* Do I hold the same opinions without realizing it?

Write down each example you can think of in which that inner part of you represented by the dream image has been operating itself in your waking life.[9]

RECORD THE DREAMS YOU HAVE WHILE WORKING WITH THIS CHAPTER.

Initiation and Descent

When we enter a forest phase in our lives we enter a period of wandering and a time of potential soul growth. Here it is possible to find what we have been cut off from, to "remember" a once vital aspect of ourselves. We may uncover a wellspring of creativity that has been hidden for decades.
—JEAN SHINODA BOLEN, *Crossing to Avalon*

Having gone through the trials to find her boon of success, the heroine reaches a point in her journey when she feels like she "has it all"—she has arrived. The love, degrees, position, prestige, and money she has sought in her focus on performance and achievement have been at least partially attained, and now she has a nagging sense of expectation. She looks around for the next mountain to climb: a new degree, a better job, another baby. Because women have a difficult time sustaining a sense of success, they are always looking for more validation. Our heroine finds yet another challenge and strives to attain her goal once again.

> *My life has been one long descent into respectability.*
> —MANDY RICE DAVIES

Eventually, after many years, this pursuit of success begins to feel like a betrayal of herself, and our heroine experiences a growing sense of spiritual aridity. She feels sucked dry, brittle, and disconnected from herself; her river of creativity has dried up. She asks herself, "What have I lost?" but hears no answer; she silenced her intuition years ago. She tries to nurture herself but finds that the resources she once turned to no longer sustain her because she has become a different person. She has dreams with recurring themes of loss—her wallet, her keys, her credit cards, her car. She dreams of becoming homeless and wandering aimlessly.

She feels betrayed not only by herself but also by the cultural mind that encouraged her to be a good girl and told her that if she trusted goal-oriented masculine thinking, her heroic efforts would be rewarded. She now feels utterly alone and deprived of comfort—but she is at a very important place in her journey: When a woman takes the time to examine her life and stops *doing,* she must learn how to simply be comfortable with *herself.* Learning how to *be* rather than *do* is not a luxury; it is a discipline. The heroine must listen carefully to her true inner voice, and that means silencing the other voices anxious to tell her what to do. She must be willing to hold the tension until the new form of her identity emerges. Anything less than patient containment aborts the emerging growth, denies the incipient change, and reverses the potential transformation. She must hold the darkness of not knowing what is next. Marion Woodman says it best when she writes:

> It takes a strong ego to hold the darkness, wait, hold the tension, waiting for we know not what. But if we can hold long enough, a tiny light is conceived in the dark unconscious, and if we can wait and hold, in its own time it will be born in its full radiance. The ego then has to be loving enough to receive the gift and nourish it with the best food that new life may eventually transform the whole personality.[1]

The spiritual aridity experienced in this phase of the journey eventually leads to an initiation and descent. The Descent is characterized as a journey to the underworld, the dark night of the soul, the belly of the whale, the meeting of the dark goddess—or simply as depression. It is usually precipitated by a life-changing loss. Experiencing the death of one's child, parent, or spouse with whom one's life and identity have been closely intertwined may mark the beginning of a descent. A divorce, a life-threatening illness or accident, the loss of self-confidence or livelihood, relocation, the inability to finish a degree, a confrontation with the grasp of an addiction, or a broken heart—any serious emotional challenge—can open the space for dismemberment and descent. The midlife passage, which I will say more about later, can also be viewed as a descent.

There seem to be certain stages that we go through in a descent. At first we feel confused or disoriented by sudden suffering, loss, pain, or an inexplicable experience. We feel out of sorts, powerless, and irritable. The irritability leads to feelings of alienation and disillusionment, and we begin to blame others for our pain. We eventually move into anger, rage, grief, and despair.

Any woman who has been through a divorce has experienced the stages of a descent. When my husband and I first separated, I felt disoriented by the change in our daily schedule. No longer did he call me from work, come home for dinner, compare the day's events with me. He wasn't there to hold me as I fell asleep at night or for me to hold when I awoke in the morning. I felt powerless to change the situation, and I pleaded with him to come home. The more powerless I felt to effect any change, the more irritable I became. Increasingly I felt disillusioned with the advice I had received from my therapist and friends and silently blamed them for supporting the split. Eventually, I was left with only anger, grief, and never-ending despair. What had I done and *why?* How had my world turned upside down overnight?

> *When a woman is "doing too much," it is a cry for help. Her only way of asking for support is to endlessly give the support she herself desperately needs.*
> —JOHN GRAY

When we have these feelings of grief and despair, we are in the underworld. In the underworld, there is no sense of time; time is endless, and you cannot rush your stay. There is no morning, afternoon, evening, or night. It is densely dark and unforgiving. This all-pervasive darkness is cold and bone-chilling. In the great myths of goddesses who have made the descent, like the Greek Persephone and the Sumerian Inanna, one's time in the darkness knows no limits. There are no easy answers in the underworld and no quick way out even for the immortal. Silence pervades when the wailing ceases. One is naked and walks on the bones of the dead.

To the outside world a woman who has begun her descent is preoccupied, sad, and inaccessible. Her tears often have no name, but they are ever-present, whether she cries or not. She cannot be comforted, and she feels utterly abandoned. She forgets things; she chooses not to see friends. She curls up in a ball on the couch or refuses to come out of her room. She digs in the earth or walks in the woods. The mud and trees become her companions. She enters a period of voluntary isolation, seen as a loss of her senses by her family and friends.

A woman must move down into the very depths of her being if she is to reclaim the parts of herself that were split off when she rejected the mother and shattered the mirror of the feminine. In this grueling process she experiences a loss of identity, a falling away of the perimeters of a known role, and an accompanying fear. She may feel dried up, raw, and devoid of sexuality or experience the gut-wrenching pain of being turned inside-out. And she may spend a long time there in the dark, waiting while life goes on up above. This breakdown of known roles, of the old myth, becomes a breakthrough that initiates a transitional stage between two periods of development. This initiation is experienced as a death so that the heroine can be reborn. She is caught between identities.

The descent is a sacred journey; we all try to avoid it, but at some point in our lives we journey to our depths. Although it is a painful journey, it invariably strengthens a woman and clarifies her sense of self. Something may be left behind or sacrificed, but it is not so much a sacrifice as it is a transformation. A woman returns to the light with unknown and as yet inexperienced potentialities that were hidden in her unconscious. So many women experience a descent at midlife that I wish to address the specifics of that here.

DESCENT AT MIDLIFE

Somewhere in her late thirties or early forties, a woman may begin to feel a nagging sense of loss. She doesn't feel as attractive, sexy, or sure of herself as she did in her earlier adulthood. The established role of spouse, mother, or career woman is beginning to shift, and the changes occurring in her body are seen as a betrayal. A woman who has been intensely involved in mothering, regardless of her involvement in her career, begins to panic as she foresees the empty nest. If she was overprotective or had an overinvolved relationship with her children—as many of the mothers of this generation have—she is likely to suffer depression and confusion as her mothering role comes to an end. No longer defined by the needs of her children, she looks longingly at soccer fields on which these children no longer play and sees an empty space she has to fill herself.

Going into the forest requires us to let go of our old ways and identities; we shed defenses, ingrained habits, and attitudes, which opens us up to new possibilities and depth.
—JEAN SHINODA BOLEN

For most fathers' daughters, whose primary focus has often been work and career, the realization that they are not going to birth a child brings a profound sense of deprivation. For so many centuries, recognition of a woman's power has been confined to her ability to give birth, so those women who choose not to actualize this potential often, though not always, feel an archetypal loss.

Midlife can be a time of tremendous emotional tumult as a woman faces the lost dreams, disappointments, and rejections that come with living a full life. Her tolerance to stress decreases as the emergence of unfamiliar fears begins to increase. Memories of childhood emotional, physical, or sexual abuse surface, and depression and rage settle in. She feels sad, stymied, at a standstill. Her memory becomes clouded, her concentration dim. For the first time in her life, perhaps, she cries at the drop of a hat. Gail Sheehy reports that 50 percent of the seven thousand women she interviewed for her book *New Passages* suffered at least one major depression during their mid-to late forties.[2] Sheehy observes that most of these depressions had more to do with the bodily reality of changes occurring in the reproductive system than with the end of a particular social role.

The physical changes that occur during midlife feel like a betrayal: the humiliation of sagging tits, midriff bulge, kimono arms, cessation of blood flow, loss of muscle tone, hot flashes, night sweats, whiskers, wrinkles, and gray and thinning hair seem to all occur at once. Heart palpitations, mood swings, and insomnia are not far behind. Weight gain, loss of libido, and dryness of the vaginal wall make many women fear the loss of their sexuality in the middle years.

The problem at midlife is not so much that a woman no longer feels sexual desire but that she fears she is losing her ability to arouse sexual desire in others. It is her feminine power that is at stake, not her sexual capacity. In some cases, the pain and anger that erupt over this awareness of decline can even increase sexual desire and activity. It is not necessarily sexual hunger that drives a woman to more activity but a desperate need to try to prove to herself that she still has power over men and can still compete sexually with others. The extreme jealousy of younger women that occurs in midlife is related to feelings of the loss of power associated with the loss of fertility and sexual appeal as well as to this culture's veneration of youth.[3] In her wonderful book *Positive Aging: Every Woman's Quest for Wisdom and Beauty,* Dr. Karen Kaigler-Walker writes:

Even if we have expectations of aging in grace and wisdom, we have precious few socially acclaimed examples of how a venerated older woman might look. I recall a group of us sitting around a table, passing around a bottle of wine, and finally coming to the conclusion that regardless of what they accomplish, fifty-year-old women win society's acclaim only when they still look thirty-five. No standards exist for the attractive forty, fifty, sixty, or seventy-year-old who actually looks her age.[4]

Loss and humiliation are the central themes during this stage of midlife; often this is the first time a woman experiences loss of control over her life. A parent becomes sick and she finds herself immediately thrown into the dilemma of how to care for this aging loved one until his or her death. She loses her job through downsizing or finds herself without economic security. Her spouse leaves her through divorce or death; she loses a sibling or child through serious illness, drug addiction, or an accident. A life-threatening illness or life circumstance makes her face her own mortality. She finds herself "wandering for seven years in the forest," undergoing an initiation process of the soul, facing all the aspects of her wounded, disheveled self that she has projected onto her parents, spouse, or others.

Women don't have hot flashes, they have power surges.

THE MYTH OF DEMETER AND PERSEPHONE

I dream that I sit at the well with Demeter and watch our tears pierce the surface of the water.

The Homeric myth of Demeter and Persephone has all the elements of the Descent, particularly at midlife.

One day Kore (later called Persephone), daughter of Demeter, goddess of the grain, was gathering flowers in a meadow with her companions, the motherless maidens Artemis and Athena. She was attracted to a beautiful narcissus with one hundred blossoms. When she reached over to pick it, the earth opened up and from deep within appeared Hades in a golden chariot pulled by four black horses. He grabbed Kore and took her with him to the underworld.

Demeter heard Kore's cries and rushed to find her. With burning torches, she searched for nine days and nine nights over land and sea for her daughter, never stopping to eat, sleep, or bathe in her frantic search. But no one could tell her what had happened to Kore. At dawn on the tenth day, Hecate, goddess of the dark moon and of the crossroads, came to Demeter and told her that she had also heard Kore's cry and knew that she had been abducted. She had not seen who had abducted her but had heard her cry. She suggested that together they go to Helios, god of the sun, which they did, and Helios told them that Hades had kidnapped Kore and taken her to the underworld to be his bride. He then told Demeter that the abduction and rape of Kore had been sanctioned by Zeus, Kore's father and the brother of Hades. Helios told Demeter to stop weeping and accept what had happened.

Demeter was furious. She felt betrayed by her consort Zeus and could not be comforted. She left Mount Olympus, disguised as an old woman, and wandered unrecognized throughout the countryside and cities. While Demeter grieved, there was no growth upon the land; it lay barren and bleak.

When Demeter reached Eleusis, she sat down near the well exhausted and grief-stricken. She stared into the well and tears fell from her eyes into the water. Daughters of the ruler of Eleusis saw Demeter at the well and were drawn to her by her beauty and presence. She told them she was looking for work as a nursemaid, and they brought her home to their mother, Metanira, to take care of their baby brother Demophon.

Demeter fed the baby ambrosia and secretly held him in a fire to make him immortal. One night, Metanira saw what Demeter was doing and screamed in fear for her son. Demeter was furious. She rose to her full height, revealing her identity and divine beauty, and berated Metanira for her stupidity. In that moment, Demeter remembered who she was, and her presence filled the house with light and fragrance. Demeter commanded that a temple be built for her, and there she sat alone with her grief for Kore. Since Demeter was the goddess of grain and the harvest, while she mourned nothing grew on the earth. Famine spread and the Olympian gods and goddesses received no offerings or sacrifices from the people. Each went to Zeus to implore his help. Finally Zeus sent his messenger Iris to ask Demeter to come back (to her senses). Demeter refused and made it abundantly clear that nothing would grow again until Kore was returned to her.

Zeus responded. He sent Hermes, messenger of the gods, to command Hades to send Kore back to Demeter so that she would abandon her anger and restore growth and fertility on the earth. Kore made ready to return to earth, but first Hades gave her pomegranate seeds, which, in her haste to return to her mother, she ate.

> As Demeter sank into her grief, so every time we are shocked out of some happy identification with another, which we have fondly imagined to be an unbreakable state, we are beset by the temptation to this surrender, to this despairing search for that which has been lost, demanding that it be restored to us exactly as it was, without any effort to discover the meaning of the experience.
> —HELEN LUKE

Hermes returned Kore to her mother, who was overjoyed to see her. Kore ran joyously into her mother's arms, and then Demeter asked her if she had eaten anything in the underworld. Kore replied that during all of her time in the underworld, she had eaten nothing except the pomegranate seeds upon her return.

Demeter told her that had she not eaten the seed of Hades, she could have stayed with her mother always—but because she had eaten the seed, she would have to return to the underworld for a third of the year, during which time the earth would lie fallow. She could stay with her mother for the remainder of the year, during which time the earth would bear fruit. From that day forward, Kore was called Persephone. After mother and daughter were reunited, Hecate came and kissed Persephone, and became her companion. Demeter restored fertility and growth to the earth and spring burst forth.

Many women feel like Demeter during a descent, particularly one that concurs with the midlife passage. It is as if their youth, that young part of themselves, like the virgin Kore, has been abducted, and no matter how much they yearn for its return, it is gone. It disappeared while they weren't watching. While a woman experiences this loss, nothing grows around her. For nine days and nine nights (the symbolic *nine* of pregnancy), Demeter searches in grief and fear without understanding what has happened. She has lost the young and carefree part of herself; her fertility has dried up, and she sits by the deep well of her emotions and weeps. Her focus turns inward.

The reward for attention is always healing. . . . More than anything else, attention is an act of connection.
—JULIA CAMERON

The challenge here for the midlife woman is to keep the torches burning, like Demeter, and to try to bring the light of understanding to what is happening to her. If she merely demands that youth be restored to her—through hormones and elective surgery—without trying to discover the significance of this life passage, she learns nothing. She must find meaning in the experience to be reborn.

During this time a woman cannot abandon herself to self-pity; she must remain responsive to her job, her family, other people. In the myth, Demeter goes to the well and draws on the wisdom of the waters of the unconscious. She offers her services as a nursemaid to care for another woman's child. The woman who is in a descent must listen carefully to messages from her unconscious in her dreams and nurture the new growth within her. We desperately cling to the status quo, but the change has already occurred and we cannot go back.

First, transformation occurs in the unconscious, and only later do we become conscious of it.

For her part, Persephone is pulled out of a daughter psychology away from her mother and enters her own descent. There she assimilates the teachings of the underworld, just before she is to return, by eating the seed of Hades. She returns to her mother but is no longer merged with her mother; she has a new sense of herself and a new name, having gone through an initiation in the underworld. She has taken the seed of the dark into herself and can now give birth to her own personality. No one can take the journey to the underworld and remain unchanged:

> Any breakthrough of new consciousness, though it may have been maturing for months or years out of sight, comes through a building up of tension that reaches a breaking point. If the man or woman stands firm with courage, the breakdown becomes a breakthrough into a surge of new life. If she cannot stand it and settles for an evasion, then she will regress into neurosis.[5]

In the last part of the myth, Persephone and Demeter are joined by Hecate. The three parts of the feminine—maiden, mother, and crone—are united. They no longer merge or fight or cling possessively to each other but are united—as one.

THE DESCENT OF INANNA

Another myth that is very important to a woman's understanding of her own descent is the Descent of Inanna. In this myth, written, on clay tablets in the third millennium B.C.E., Inanna, the ancient Sumerian goddess of heaven and earth, makes a conscious decision to travel to the underworld to witness the funeral rites of Gugalanna, husband of her sister Ereshkigal, queen of the underworld. Unlike Persephone, Inanna is not abducted into the underworld; she *chooses* to make the journey, shedding her identification with the masculine, dying to an old way of being, and waiting for rebirth. She descends, submits, and dies; hers is not a passive passage, for she expresses an active willingness to receive and grow.[6]

Before she makes her descent, Inanna instructs Ninshubur, her faithful servant, to appeal to the father gods, Enlil, Nanna, and Enki, for help in securing her release if she does not return within three days. She asks Ninshubur to act as "fair witness" to her descent.

Inanna begins her descent, and at the first gate to the netherworld, she is stopped and asked to declare herself by the gatekeeper Neti. When Neti informs Ereshkigal, queen of the underworld, that Inanna has asked for admission to witness the funeral of Gugalanna, Ereshkigal becomes furious. She insists that Inanna be treated according to the same laws and rites as for anyone else entering her kingdom. She must remove her royal garments and enter the underworld naked and bowed low.

To descend of your own volition, to let go of all earthly trappings, to let go of "doing," this implies inner power. [Inanna] had sufficient inner resources to risk such a journey.
—DIANE WOLKSTEIN

The gatekeeper follows these orders and has Inanna remove one piece of her magnificent regalia at each of the seven gates. She strips herself bare, divesting herself of everything that has defined her in the upper world at each gate. When she arrives in the underworld, Ereshkigal fixes her with the eye of death. She strikes her dead and hangs her corpse on a peg to rot.

When Inanna fails to return after three days, Ninshubur begins to lament and beats her drum, circling the houses of the gods. She goes to Enlil, the highest god of sky and earth, and to Nanna, the moon god and Inanna's father, but both refuse to meddle in the ways of the underworld. Finally Enki, the god of waters and wisdom, ruler of the flow of sea and rivers, hears Ninshubur's plea and grieves for Inanna.

Enki (who could be seen as the god associated with emotions) makes two creatures, neither male nor female, called the *kalatura* and *kurgara*, from the dirt under his fingernails. He gives them both food and drink to bring to the underworld and tells them to grieve with Ereshkigal. They slip unnoticed into the underworld and comfort Ereshkigal, who is mourning over the death of her consort. She is so grateful for their empathy that she offers them a gift. They ask for Inanna's corpse, over which they sprinkle food and the water of life. Restored to life, Inanna is reminded that if she wishes to return from the underworld, she has to provide a substitute to take her place. As she returns through the seven gates to the upper world and reclaims her royal garments, demons cling to her so that they might retrieve her scapegoat. The last part of the myth involves the search for her substitute, her consort Dumuzi, who did not mourn her death but took over her throne instead.

If we look at this myth as a metaphor for our own lives, Ninshubur could be seen as the "ally within" who remains fair witness to our process, who can see and act on our behalf even when we are in deep despair. Ninshubur appeals to the sky and moon gods for help. She looks to the fathers, who seemingly have all the power but are either incapable of or unwilling to help. When we are in pain, many of us first look to the wrong sources for comfort. If we were unable to receive the nurturance and approval we needed from our parents as children, we will repeat this pattern of expecting help from those who are incapable of giving, until we learn to turn to more nourishing sources.[7]

Being stripped bare at each gate can be seen as a humiliation of the ego: a letting go of those false identities our heroic ego clings to in an effort to define ourselves in the outer world—our roles, our beliefs about ourselves, our illusions and attachments. We sacrifice these conscious outer-directed aspects of ourselves to a deeper understanding of our unconscious and feminine nature. This myth shows us also how those dark, repressed parts of ourselves can be integrated into conscious life through emotional upheavals and grief, changing our way of being in the world.[8]

The incredible part of sharing, enduring Inanna's journey, is the ascent. Having emerged from the underworld, I now feel the presence of my child self. She is calling to me, she's playing hide-and-seek with me, she's laughing.
—DIANE WOLKSTEIN

When Inanna makes her descent, Ereshkigal fixes her with the eye of death and hangs her corpse on a peg to rot. The Jungian analyst Murray Stein writes about the importance of identifying the corpse in one's life, particularly during midlife. What is the deepest cause of our sense of loss? What part of ourselves is dying? What former dream or identification of self has to be put to rest? If there is no conscious separation from this earlier identity, the corpse does not get buried but instead is hidden or propped up.[9] If we don't make this loss conscious, we persevere in holding on to an earlier pattern even after it has long outlived its usefulness and has effectively undergone demise. Sometimes we need an ally to help us identify the corpse and bury it! The nature of the loss has to be understood and experienced before a person can go through a renewal. Metaphorically, this is what happens as Inanna hangs on the peg to rot.

Ereshkigal is the part of a woman that has gone underground by splitting off in her initial separation from the feminine. She represents those qualities we repress in our attempt to fit into the dominant culture, particularly those qualities stemming from our bodily and emotional wisdom. In the myth, Ereshkigal first expresses rage, then active destructiveness, then suffering, and finally gratitude for empathic listening. In meeting the Ereshkigal aspect of oneself, a woman confronts her own unexpressed rage, denial, sadness, fear of loss, and grief. Ereshkigal demands that we look at those parts of ourselves we don't wish to see—our passivity, the disappointment or blame we project onto others, our greediness, our hubris, and so on. She is the place both of death and of new life lying dormant, the point of necessary destruction and of healing.

During the descent, a woman experiences a period of introversion or depression, a slow, painful self-pregnancy in which she scrapes away her identification with ego-consciousness and goes back to a state of body knowing that precedes words. She may feel an incredible sense of emptiness, of having been ground down and pulverized. She may feel orphaned, homeless, shunned, left behind, without value. Like both Demeter and Inanna, such a woman will bear no fruit, no product. She may feel naked and exposed, sexless, arid, and raw. She may dream of wandering in underground tunnels, subways, mazes, wombs, and tombs from which she struggles to find her way out.

In the following dream, I find myself fighting to make my way out of the descent before understanding my purpose in the underworld.

I dream that I'm with my daughter in an underground transportation tunnel. She is taking me to a place from which I have to make my return. We arrive at a place that feels very threatening. We've lost our conveyance and I see a bed that can be used as a vehicle. It has an ignition that can be lit with matches. I send my daughter off to talk to a man from whom we might be able to buy this powered bed. As I try to get to the bed to ignite, an unshaven man attempts to block me. I struggle with him and yell my daughter's name. As I wrestle with my attacker, I hear my daughter calling my name; *she* is in trouble. I get away from the man and get the bed ignited. I move it out of an old ramshackle building and head down a passageway, turning it with the weight of my body by shifting back and forth, like on a skateboard. I drive it into a square where my daughter has been assaulted by the man with whom she was negotiating the sale of the bed. I pull her onto the bed and we make our escape. She is quiet, mute, disappointed that I didn't come to her when she called. I try to explain to her that I was trying to get a vehicle to bring us to safety, but I feel like I have failed her.

In this dream, I am so focused on getting a vehicle to get out of the underground tunnel that I do not attend to my "daughter," my own new growth occurring in the underworld. I cannot stand the pain and ego humiliation I am experiencing (as I go through a second divorce). I will use any conveyance, even an old abandoned bed I have to ignite with matches, to circumvent my discomfort. I am willing to sacrifice my feeling nature in an attempt to find a heroic solution to my problem. I refuse to accept that I cannot work my will in the underworld.

This period in the "tunnel" is a core experience that allows the seeding of a new personal myth. Clarissa Pinkola Estes writes, "The breakthrough [of the new story] is experienced at the same time as a breakdown. The core experience, like every initiation, involves a wounding."[10]

If a woman can allow the descent to be a mindful initiation and see it as a sacred process, she need not become lost in the dark. She will need patience to allow herself the time and effort to discover the meaning of the experience, or else the teachings of the descent will become obscured and there will be no renewal. Most of us try to distance ourselves from the pain and ego humiliation we feel in the underworld; yet only an act of conscious, willing surrender to the process will allow transformation to occur.[11]

Returning to the myth, Ninshubur finally goes to Enki, the wily water and wisdom god who improvises what the moment needs. He creates creatures that are neither male nor female to grieve with Ereshkigal. She is in deep mourning and these asexual creatures suffer with her. They don't implore her to *do* anything; they simply allow her to *be* in her pain. They sing her lamentations with her. Ereshkigal feels heard and this allows her to accept her pain as it is—as part of life's natural process. She doesn't have to blame anyone; she can simply be with her suffering and heal naturally. This quality of empathy—of being *with* the pain—helps one to move through it. We do not know the outcome of the descent or the changes that will occur, but we do know that "finding renewal and connection with the potent forces of the underworld will involve breaking up the old pattern."[12] The birth of new life demands a sacrifice of an old way of living.

When Ereshkigal feels heard, she allows the kalatura and kurgara to restore Inanna to life. Inanna is revived with food and water to replenish her soul. She then makes her return from the underworld accompanied by demons to seek her substitute. Inanna finds Dumuzi, her consort, her equal, her beloved, sitting on her throne, unconcerned about her plight. When she sees him, she is furious, and like Ereshkigal, she fixes him with the eye of death and commands that he be taken away to the underworld. She sacrifices the one most cherished to her, which can be seen as one's favorite attitude or ideal (for example, that things will be easy and innocent).[13]

The goddess Inanna then mourns the loss of her beloved, as does Geshti-nanna, the sister of Dumuzi. Out of love and grief for her brother, Geshtinanna appeals to Inanna to let her take Dumuzi's place in the underworld. Inanna is so moved by her offer of conscious sacrifice that she allows Geshtinanna to share Dumuzi's time in the underworld; each will spend six months in the under-world and six months on earth. Geshtinanna is a wise woman who is in touch with her feelings, humble and conscious of her sacrifice. She offers herself to her friend Inanna out of love for her brother. She is willing to endure the cycle of descent-ascent-descent, ending the pattern of scapegoating by choosing to confront the underworld herself.[14]

When we return from the descent, we have to learn to hold the dark as we move forward on our journey. We must hold it with open hands, not clinging to the suffering of the descent but honoring the mystery of the descent. If we learn to hold the dark as a loved one, we can befriend the pain as we take our wisdom from it. Then we will be able to feel gratitude for its teaching. Trusting the mystery of manifestation is one of the deep teachings of the feminine journey.

In "I come from a dark house," poet Fiona O'Connell writes:

> At noon on the plains where no trees are
> the light is pitiless. Bones are there, dry,
> unnumbered, not accounted for,
> at no known time bone of God's bone,
> female bones with no memory of being
> fundament, pillar, lintel, sill, or roofbeam
> of any hut or castle, or of having
> upheld the blind truth of being
> through the times of any of our lives.
> I cannot say to these hones, scattered
> to the four corners, dispersed, and without
> recollection, "Speak to me." How would
> they read me? Nothing of me coheres.

I come from a dark house, too long shaded
for me to go out on the plains at noon.[15]

GUIDED IMAGERY: THE DESCENT

I mentioned in the introduction that women who attend workshops on the Heroine's Journey often get annoyed, judgmental, and angry on the day we begin the Descent. My caution is worth repeating here: You may find that as you work with the material in this chapter, you may want to close the book and stop the process. Don't. Be kind to yourself and take a deep breath. Make yourself a cup of tea or go for a walk. Support yourself with love and compassion. Never judge yourself. Be patient with your process and make a commitment to work through the issues of the Descent in your own timing.

The spirit, it might fly to Heaven, but the soul, it must go to its depths, to the soil of itself. Soul to soil.

—RHODA LERMAN

You may recall that in the myth of Inanna and Ereshkigal, Inanna asked her handmaiden, Ninshubur, to be fair witness to her descent and to call upon the gods if she did not return in three days. As you begin your descent to the underworld, call upon an ally part of yourself to be fair witness to your journey. This exercise is long and intensive; you may wish to do it in one session, or you might prefer to spread it out over a two-week period, completing one gate at a time.

Gabrielle Roth's *Totem* makes a good musical accompaniment for this exercise.

Now close your eyes and focus your attention on your breath. All of your attention is on the air going in and out of your nostrils. Take three deep breaths and give yourself the suggestion that with each exhalation, your body becomes more and more relaxed. Now imagine that you, like Inanna, are about to make your descent to the underworld to meet your dark sister, Ereshkigal. You prepare yourself for your journey by dressing in your finest clothes, including your crown, royal cloak, and jewels. You walk down a path that begins to spiral downward, and in the distance you see a gate of your own creation. In front of the gate awaits a gatekeeper.

As you approach, the gatekeeper looks you in the eye and asks, "What is it that you want?" You reply, "I journey to the underworld to meet my sister, the goddess Ereshkigal." The gatekeeper leaves you at the gate and goes to the underworld to announce your arrival. Ereshkigal says that you must undergo the same rites as everyone else who enters the underworld. You must arrive naked and bowed low.

The gatekeeper returns to tell you of Ereshkigal's bidding and asks you to remove your crown and veil. You reach up and take off your crown and hand it to the gatekeeper. What does the crown look like? What does it mean to you? Could it be that the crown represents your attachment to your mind and what it tells you about yourself? What does it feel like to take off your crown? Are you ready to relinquish it? The gatekeeper accepts your crown, bows low before you, and opens the gate. You cross the threshold and continue down the path, going deeper and deeper. (Pause. At this point you may wish to spend some time writing or drawing the images and insights that come to you during this first part of the exercise. Think about what you gave up and what it meant to you. If you would prefer to continue the exercise, pause before traveling to the next gate.)

At the next gate, the gatekeeper asks you to remove your necklace. What does it look like? Is it beaded, jeweled, a simple strand of silver or pearls? Is it heavy? What does it mean to you? Could it be the cultural and familial voices that told you who to be? Or perhaps it is your need for external approval? What does it feel like to release it at this point? The gatekeeper accepts the necklace, bows low before you, and opens the gate. You cross the threshold and continue down the path.

The next gatekeeper asks you to remove your outer cloak or robe. What color is it? What is its texture? How has it weighed you down? What does this cloak mean to you? Could it be your public persona—the good girl chronically smiling and performing? Or perhaps your need for power and status? How does it feel to take it off? The gatekeeper receives your cloak and opens the gate. You cross the threshold and continue your descent.

At the fourth gate, the gatekeeper asks you to remove your blouse and camisole. What color are they? What type of material? Have they protected your breasts, your heart? What do they represent to you? Could they be the ways in which you have injured your heart? Perhaps you have had negative feelings like shame, guilt, or anger for yourself. How does it feel to take them off? The gatekeeper accepts your blouse and camisole, bows low before you, and you continue on your journey.

At the next gate, the gatekeeper asks you to remove your rings and brace-lets. What do your rings look like and what do they mean to you? Who has given them to you? Perhaps your rings and bracelets represent your attachments to certain people in your life? Do they signify your role as wife, lover, daughter, sister? How do you feel as you take them off? Is it easy or difficult to relinquish them? You give them to the gatekeeper and continue on your path.

At the sixth gate, the gatekeeper asks you to remove your skirt and under-garments. What color and style is your skirt? What kind of undergarments do you wear? What meanings do your skirt and underwear hold for you? Perhaps they represent your attachment to your sexuality, or sexual wounds? The gate-keeper accepts your clothes, bows low before you, and opens the gate. You cross the threshold and continue on the spiral path, going deeper and deeper into the underworld.

At the seventh gate, the gatekeeper asks you to remove your shoes. What do your shoes look like? How do they feel? Are they comfortable? Are they a tight fit? What do they mean to you? Perhaps they represent your connection to your body and the earth, or how you move through life? Are you driven by ego demands or do you move with grace and balance? How do you feel as you relinquish your shoes? The gatekeeper takes them, bows low before you, and opens the gate. You walk forward in the darkness into the underworld to meet Ereshkigal.

Ereshkigal stands there waiting for you. Naked, you approach her cau-tiously. It is dark but you look closely, wanting to see her face. What does she look like? Who does she remind you of? Who is she? You bow down low before the Dark Goddess, aware of her power. She stares at you with a piercing gaze. You see just how much she has suffered. In that moment you know that you have abandoned her and abandoned yourself. She reaches out and fixes you with the eye of death.

She hangs you on a peg to rot. You feel your life juices draining out of you. You are nothing but a sack of bones. You feel empty and alone. You mourn and she mourns as well. You surrender. (Pause and breathe deeply with the music for several minutes. Breathe life into those parts of yourself you have rejected, discarded, abandoned. Take as much time as you need.)

Eventually you begin to feel restored. You express your gratitude and promise your dark sister that you will never abandon her again. She reminds you never to abandon yourself. How do you feel as she says this to you?

She tells you it is time to make your return. She advises you to reclaim only those parts of yourself you are willing to honor. She embraces you and asks if you are ready to leave. How do you feel as you say farewell? (Pause.)

You begin your long journey out of the underworld. The path is dark, but it spirals upward. There is a dim light glowing in the distance. A gatekeeper awaits you and hands you your shoes. As you put them on, you notice they feel different. As you pass through the gate what do you reclaim? Perhaps your positive connection to your body, your health, and the earth. (Pause.) The gatekeeper bows low and blesses your return.

At the sixth gate, the gatekeeper hands you your skirt and undergarments. As you put them on you notice how they fit. What is it you wish to reclaim? Perhaps your love and appreciation for your healthy sexuality, your certainty that you do have a choice. (Pause.) You pass through the gate and continue the journey upward.

At the next gate, the gatekeeper hands you your rings and your bracelets. You take back only those you still wish to wear. Which people and what roles do you want in your life? How does it feel to choose healthy relationships? How do you feel as you leave some behind? (Pause.) The gatekeeper bows low as you pass through the gate.

At the fourth gate, the gatekeeper hands you your camisole and blouse. Notice how much lighter they feel as you put them on. What positive feelings about yourself are you willing to reclaim? Perhaps now you will celebrate yourself as you pass through the gate. (Pause.)

You continue traveling to the third gate, where the gatekeeper hands you your cloak or robe. You put it around your shoulders and spin in a circle. You reclaim who you want to be in the world as an authentic person, not the persona you once wore. The gatekeeper bows low before you and you journey to the next gate. (Pause.)

At the second gate, the gatekeeper puts your necklace into your hands. What does it feel like? How does it look? As you clasp it around your neck, what do you reclaim? Perhaps you find your distinct voice. You speak aloud positive affirmations, such as "[your name], you are strong, you are loved." The gatekeeper smiles and opens the gate.

At the final gate, the gatekeeper awaits you with your crown. As you place it on your head, you feel different. The competing voices of your mind have become still. The gatekeeper acknowledges you as queen and bows low before you. As you cross the threshold to the upper world, you have a deeper understanding about yourself and appreciation for your journey. You have made your descent and returned with more of you intact. You have enormous gratitude for Ereshkigal, your dark sister.

Walk, dance, and celebrate your new being.

QUESTIONS FOR WRITING AND REFLECTION

* Who was your ally? Did your ally accompany you on your journey or wait for your return?
* Did you recognize any of the gatekeepers from your waking life or dreams? Were the gatekeepers aspects of yourself? What function did the gatekeepers serve?
* What was your experience of being with Ereshkigal, the dark sister? Who was she? Was it hard to leave her? What promise did you make to her, to yourself?
* At each step of the journey, what did you give up, what did you reclaim, and what did it mean to you?

Write, draw, paint, or record your descent and return.

WRITING EXERCISE

Identify the physical and emotional losses you have experienced during your life, your disappointments and unrealized dreams, and your roles and relationships that have been altered or have come to an end. How have you coped with these?

SEVERANCE RITUAL: LOSS BUNDLES

Ritual is one of the faculties we have, like dreaming, that enable us to set up a flow of communication between the conscious mind and the unconscious. A highly conscious ritual sends a powerful message back to the unconscious, causing changes to take place at the deep levels where our attitudes and values

One thing that our unconscious will not tolerate is evasion of responsibility. The unconscious pushes us into one suffering after another, one impossible mess after another, until we are finally willing to wake up, see that it is we who are choosing these impossible paths, and take responsibility for our own decisions.
—ROBERT A. JOHNSON

originate. Ritual provides deep communication with our soul, reawakening our spiritual lives and our sense of awe.[16]

For this ritual you will need paper, pens, strips of black cloth, and red yarn or thread. You may choose to do this ritual in a group or by yourself with a friend who is willing to be fair witness. You may wish to clear the ritual area first by cleaning it, burning sage to purify it, calling upon spiritual guidance, and making clear your intention to create sacred space.

Now that you have completed the exercise of the descent and have examined repetitive behaviors or attitudes that you have outgrown, we are going to ritualize the process. You have already identified the physical and emotional losses you have experienced throughout your life, your disappointments and unrealized dreams, and your roles and relationships that have been altered or have come to an end. At this point, it is important for you to recognize any pattern in your life that no longer serves you. Perhaps it is one of attachment, blame, anger, resentment, living in fantasy, or feeling trapped by your own passivity.

Write down the repetitive patterns you see in your life. What are you now willing to release so you no longer have to carry it forward in your life? Choose one that best speaks to what needs to be severed for you to continue your growth and development.

Write that on a small piece of paper and bind it with the cloth and red thread. As you bind it, know deeply in your heart that you are willing to let it go. Know also that your determination will be tested; it always is when you do a ritual of severance. Pay attention to how you are tested in the coming days and weeks. Now, when you are ready, speak your intention aloud in the manner of the examples below, and then burn your loss bundle or bury it.

I, your name, am now willing to release my dependence on my husband and my unwillingness to fully embrace my own destiny.

I, _____, am now willing to stop blaming the men in my life for the shame that I feel in my body.

I, _____, am now willing to release my fear of and resentment about being swallowed by my mother.

I, _____, am now willing to release my yearning for the unavailable man.

I, _____, am now willing to release my children to live their own lives.

CORPSE EXERCISE

This exercise is another way to release a harmful pattern or attitude that causes you pain. Fashion a corpse figure out of clay and other natural elements, such as sticks, stones, and grasses. While you are making it, identify the exact and deepest source of your pain and sense of loss and put that into your clay figure. Perhaps you have blamed yourself for not being able to bear a child or for not achieving the career goals you once held for yourself. Be conscious of what you are willing to release as you fashion the figure.

Let the corpse figure dry and seal it with white glue such as Elmer's, covering the entire surface. Paint it or decorate it as you wish. Then create a ceremony to begin the process of letting go by grieving, mourning, and burying the figure in the earth. As you did before in creating ceremony, clear the ritual space first by cleaning it, burning sage to purify it, calling upon spiritual guidance, and stating your intention in laying this loss to rest. It is important that the nature of the loss be understood and worked through before a person can go on.

DREAM INTERPRETATION

The Jungian analyst Robert A. Johnson suggests that in interpreting your dreams, you ask yourself the following questions:

* What is the central most important message this dream is trying to communicate to me?
* What is it advising me to do?
* What is the overall meaning of the dream for my life?
* What is the most important insight this dream is trying to get across to me?[17]

Write down your interpretation and see if it makes sense to you. Does it correspond with anything that has been going on in your life?

Choose an interpretation that challenges your existing ideas, rather than one that merely repeats what you already think you know. Sometimes you will have dreams that send you the same basic message over and over; in this case, it is probably because you don't understand the message or refuse to put it into practice.[18] What is the message that you don't want to hear?

Avoid an interpretation that inflates your ego or shifts responsibility away from yourself. Dreams do not tell you how another person is wrong or needs to change; your dreams are concerned with *you*. They show you what you need to face or the areas of your life where you need to change.

Learn to live with the dream over time. Usually a dream can be understood in relation to specific events in your inner life in recent days, but sometimes you may have a "big" dream. This type of dream will give you a glimpse of what has happened in the past, what is happening at present, and what may take place in the future.[19] Sometimes these dreams appear in a series of three.

At times you will be unable to find an interpretation to a dream that feels right to you; be patient with the ambiguity of the dream just as you have to be patient with the uncertainty of life.[20] As you live with the dream its meaning will become clearer.

It is helpful to review your dreams at least once a year to see how they have been maps for your inner growth and outer life.

RECORD THE DREAMS YOU HAVE WHILE WORKING WITH THIS CHAPTER.

4

Urgent Yearning to Reconnect with the Feminine

The waiting of the feminine is there and was always there, born with the feminine, always alive in the feminine. It was the waiting of creation itself, the waiting which is at the heart of time where out of a longing the stars are made and the child is formed and born. How could one not have known that all the living and growing and all the light and shining things coming out of the darkness at the beginning were made out of this waiting?
—LAURENS VAN DER POST, *About Blady*

After a woman has made her descent and severed her identity as a spiritual daughter of the patriarchy, there is an urgent yearning to reconnect with the feminine, whether that takes the form of an old woman, the Goddess, or her little girl within. This desire to know the feminine on a deep level is illustrated in the dream below, in which the central figure is an archetypal wise woman preparing food. The dreamer brings her an offering of a chalice-like vessel, a symbol of the creative feminine womb. She recognizes and honors the Great Mother and receives her nurturance. There is communion with the other women.

> I dream that I board an old clipper ship or fishing vessel where an ancient woman is preparing a meal on a raised wooden plank in the center of the ship. There are two younger women standing on either side of her, assisting. I carry something aboard that looks like a covered urn

or vessel and give it to her. I eat the food she prepares with my fingers. The other women pick up the food she prepares with pita bread. The dream feels like an ancient ritual.

During this stage of the Heroine's Journey, a woman desires to be mentored by older women, to celebrate the feminine in ritual with women, to attend to the rhythms of her own body, to attune to the cycles of nature and the moon, and to spend time in nature. It is a time to listen to her dreams and intuition and to express her creativity. It is a time during which a woman becomes more aware of her feminine consciousness and defines it for herself. She also recognizes her body as the sacred container of her soul.

She longs to develop those parts of herself that have gone underground while she was on her heroic quest. If a woman has ignored her feelings while serving the needs of family or community, she may now slowly begin to reclaim her emotions. If she has spent many years fine-tuning her intellect and her command of the material world while ignoring the subtleties of her bodily knowing, she may now be reminded that her mind, body, and spirit are one.

Many women have experienced so much discomfort living inside a female body that they have abused it with food, alcohol, drugs, exercise, or overwork to exorcise the unease of being born female. If a daughter became male-identified in an effort to please her father, like I did, she emphasized the development of her mind and intellect and rejected (in varying degrees of awareness—for example, constant self-criticism is a form of rejection) her female body. She forgot how to listen to its wants and needs. The body is intelligent; it knows when it is hungry, thirsty, needs rest, wants to exercise, wants sex, doesn't want sex, and is out of balance. Many of us, however, have been trained to ignore and override its communication.

If a woman's mother did not relate to her own body as female, or made disparaging remarks about her sexuality or the sexuality of other women, she was probably unable to cherish the female body of her baby daughter.[1] Some women tell their daughters horror stories about their first sexual experience or about the pains of childbirth, so many girls fear sexuality, loathe their bodies, and slowly cut themselves off from their instinctual knowing.

As a woman returns from the descent, however, she takes back her body, and in this act of reclamation, she not only takes back her personal physical form but also embodies the sacredness of the feminine for all of us. She begins to make conscious its needs. Through conscious nutrition, exercise, bathing, rest, healing, lovemaking, and birthing, she reminds us of the sanctity of the feminine. For many women, including myself, the most sacred moments have been physical ones: being held, making love, nursing a child. Nothing brought me closer to the ecstasy of the sacred than giving birth.

Marion Woodman writes, "The feminine leads us to the sharp edge of experience. There we have to feel our feelings in our bodies; there our secrets become visible in the darkened, unvisited corners of our psyches. Claiming the unswept corners of our psyches leads us to compassion for ourselves and for others. Knowing we have done our best and it simply wasn't enough opens our hearts to other human beings whose best has likewise failed. The mind has its logic; the heart alone can know wisdom, bridge chasms, make peace."[2]

BODY-SPIRIT SPLIT

Historically, the connection between body and soul was destroyed with the overthrow of the Mother Goddess. It is only now, with the threat of massive destruction of Mother Earth, that this connection is being reclaimed. When humankind forgot the sanctity of the earth and began to worship its gods in churches and temples instead of in groves and on hilltops, it lost the sacred "I–Thou" relationship with nature. We lost the sense of sacredness embodied in all living beings, trees, rocks, oceans, four-leggeds, birds, children, men, and women. With this disregard for the sanctity of nature came the denial of the sanctity of the body. It was not always this way.

When the body of woman was the equivalent of the body of the Goddess, a woman was the container for the miracle of life. During the Middle Ages, and

It was not for seeking knowledge that Eve was ejected from the Garden of Eden; it was for seeking her own soul.
—SUZANNE BUSSARD

particularly since the Industrial Revolution and its deification of the machine, the physical body of both women and men, like Mother Earth, has been sexually and physically abused. The body has been pushed beyond limits of strength and endurance and made to conform to cultural expectations of size, shape, and beauty in the interest of serving human greed. The denigration of the female body has been expressed in cultural and religious taboos surrounding menstruation, childbirth, and menopause; it is also reflected in mounting statistics documenting rape, incest, and pornography. The sacredness of the female body, the recognition of sacredness in matter, was lost as people began to worship the father gods. The reverence and fertility once accorded a menstruating woman went underground along with the Goddess. In her absence, some women forgot the deep wisdom of their female body and the mysteries of feminine sexuality. Women *know* with their bodies.

Jean Shinoda Bolen says, "When we know something in our bodies as well as with our mind and hearts, then we know something deeply about ourselves, and it is this dimension that has been out of balance in our Christian civilization and our Christian-influenced psychology. It has been so much a father psychology as well as a father theology, where mind, interpretations, and the word are the transformative experience, and that's not true for women."[3]

As archeologists uncover ancient cultures based on the life-giving principles of the Goddess, women have begun to reclaim the power and dignity once accorded them when the role of woman was to protect human life and the sacredness of nature. Ancient images of strong women giving birth offer a model for participation in society and represent a time when one's inner life was as valued and as real as one's interaction with the external world. Becoming aware of the Goddess in everyday life involves uncovering our tacit approval of and unconscious service to the patriarchy in our personal lives and work situations and bringing ourselves into right relationship with the Earth. This translates to listening to ourselves and acting on our truth, being more attentive and responsible to the present instead of focusing on five-year plans, bringing feminine values of cooperation instead of competition into the home and workplace, and developing relationships with men and women that allow them to be all that they are.

The original separation from the feminine occurred when the primacy of the Goddess gave way to subordination to male gods.
—JUDY CHICAGO

WOMAN AS CREATOR

A woman who has made the descent has experienced the devouring, destroyer aspect of the feminine, which is in the service of the death and renewal of herself. After the dryness and aridity experienced during this separation from life "above," she yearns for the moist, green, juicy aspect of the creative feminine. A woman who has felt cut off from her feminine nature may slowly begin to reclaim who she is as she feels her creativity begin to flow. This renewal may occur in the garden, in the kitchen, in decorating the home, in relationship, in weaving, writing, or dance. Her sense of aesthetics and sensuality come alive as she is refreshed by color, smell, taste, touch, and sound. Antonia, a woman in her early forties, had the following dream during this period:

> I am in my house with my tai chi teacher. He opens my closet and there is a huge, beautiful white tiger sitting in the closet in its native environment. The environment is lush and green. My tai chi teacher says, "You shouldn't have a wild animal with you; it can be dangerous." I reply, "I didn't bring it here with me; it materializes anytime I am focused and concentrated."

Antonia woke up feeling proud of the white tiger. The lush dream environment of the tiger indicates the quality of the feminine that is verdant, alive, and deeply nurturing. This is the quality we long for as we return from the descent. The dreamer does not search for this type of healing power; it is available to her every time she is open and focused. She need not worry that this power is dangerous to herself or others; when it is concentrated, it is deeply nurturing.

This speaks to the quality of the feminine that allows things to happen in the natural cycle of things. People who work at deep levels of the unconscious in dreams, in therapy, and in the creative process know that there are phases of both quietude and renewal and that these must be respected, protected, and given time. Daughters of the father, like myself, have a difficult time *allowing* things to happen. We think we have to *make* things happen. Waiting for an outcome and the uncertainty of the result can create enormous anxiety for someone like me. But I also know that I cannot force birth. I must endure the process because I am gestating something new.

The following tale of the Handless Maiden illustrates the necessity of allowing time for renewal after a woman has been cut off from her creative feminine nature and made her Descent. She must go inward, or "wander in the forest," to reclaim the parts of herself that have been sacrificed—her sexuality, creativity, intuition, her potential as a woman. Only then can she give birth to something new.

THE HANDLESS MAIDEN

In Grimms' tale of sacrifice and loss between a father and his daughter, a miller who has fallen on hard times is tricked by a stranger in the woods into exchanging "what stands behind his mill" for a treasure that will restore the miller's wealth.[4] The stranger says, "Why do you plague yourself with cutting wood? I will make you rich, if you will promise me what is standing behind your mill."[5] The miller agrees to this bargain, thinking that what stands behind his mill is an apple tree. The stranger says he will return in three years to collect his due. When the miller returns home from the woods, he sees untold wealth pouring out of his house, but when he tells his wife about the stranger he made the bargain with, she upbraids him for his foolishness. "That must have been the Devil!" she exclaims in horror. "He did not mean the apple tree, but our *daughter,* who was standing behind the mill sweeping the yard."[6]

The daughter has three years before the Devil can claim her and during that time she lives a pious life. The day the Devil comes to fetch her, she bathes, dresses in white, and then draws a circle of chalk around herself. When the Devil sees the pail of water she used to wash herself, he cannot approach her and angrily says to the miller: "Take all water away from her, that she may no longer be able to wash herself, for otherwise I have no power over her."[7]

The miller complies in fear, and the next morning the Devil comes again to claim the daughter. This time she has wept on her hands, so once again he is unable to approach her. Furious, the Devil tells the miller to cut off his daughter's hands or he will take the miller himself. The father is appalled by this request, but nevertheless agrees to do so. In fear and shame he goes to her and says: "My child, if I do not cut off both your hands, the Devil will carry me away, and in my terror I have promised to do it. Help me in my need, and forgive me the harm I do you." The daughter replies: "Dear father, do with me what you will, I am your child."⁸ The maiden lays down her hands on the chopping block and her father severs them. The Devil comes again in the morning, but she has wept all night on the stumps and, once again, he cannot approach her. Having failed the third time, the Devil is obliged to relinquish all rights to the daughter.

The miller tells his daughter that because he has received great wealth as a result of her sacrifice, he will care for her well. She declines his offer, telling him that she can no longer stay with him. "Here I cannot stay, I will go forth, compassionate people will give me as much as I require."⁹ She asks that her maimed hands be bound to her back and she leaves.

The maiden walks and walks until nightfall, when she comes to a royal garden filled with pear trees. She cannot enter the garden, however, because it is surrounded by a moat. By this time she is very hungry, so she falls to her knees to pray, and a spirit comes to her and dries up the moat. The maiden walks over to one of the pear trees and, standing there with her hands bound to her back, puts her lips to the fruit of one of the golden pears and eats it. All of this is witnessed by a gardener who watches in awe, recognizing the magic of the spirit who guards the maiden.

The next morning the king comes to his garden to count his golden pears, and when he finds one missing, he asks the gardener what happened. The gardener replies that a spirit drained the moat and another spirit without hands ate the pear. The king decides to keep watch that night with the gardener and to bring along a magician who can communicate with spirits.

That night the three men wait under the tree, and at midnight the maiden and the spirit return. The maiden once again eats one of the golden pears, and the magician approaches her and asks if she is mortal or spirit. The maiden replies that she is a mortal forsaken by all but God, and the king rushes to her and says, "I shall not forsake you." He takes her to his royal palace, has a pair of silver hands made for her and fastened to her arms, and marries her.

After a year the king has to go off to war and leaves his young queen, whom he dearly loves, in the care of his mother. "If she gives birth to a child, send me a message right away," he says.

The young queen gives birth to a son, and the king's mother sends a messenger to the king to give him the good news. On the way, the messenger rests near a river, and while he is asleep the Devil comes and exchanges the letter for another in which he has written that the queen has given birth to a child that is half dog.

The king is horrified by the message but writes back that his mother must take good care of the queen during this terrible time. The messenger once again falls asleep near the river and the Devil changes the letter to "Kill the queen and her child."

The old mother is stunned by the king's letter and sends him another message to confirm. But she never receives a different answer because the Devil keeps intercepting the messages at the river and changing them. The last letter from the king instructs her to keep the tongue and eyes of the queen to prove that she has been killed.

The old mother, who has become very attached to the young queen, cannot stand to have her killed. She has a doe sacrificed instead, keeping its tongue and eyes, and she helps the young queen bind her infant to her breast and tearfully bids her goodbye.

The young queen wanders until she comes to a great wild forest, and she picks her way along the path. At nightfall the same spirit who had come to her years before in the king's garden comes to her and leads her to a small house where she is welcomed by forest folk. The queen stays there for seven years and lives life with her child. Her hands gradually grow back, first as little baby hands, then as little girl's hands, and finally as woman's hands.[10]

During this time the king returns from war and his mother reproaches him with his letters, saying, "How could you have me kill two innocents?" She shows him the tongue and the eyes he had requested in his letter, and the king begins to grieve inconsolably for his wife and son. He weeps so bitterly that his mother takes pity on him and tells him that these are the eyes and tongue of a doe and that she has sent his wife and child off into the forest.

The king then vows to travel as far as the sky is blue, neither eating nor drinking until he finds his wife and child. He searches for seven years, looking everywhere, fasting the entire time, sustained by a greater force. At last he comes to the little house in the woods and is welcomed in to rest. He looks like a wild man, his hair and beard matted and long. He lays down and puts a handkerchief over his face. As he sleeps the handkerchief slips off his face, and when he awakes he sees a beautiful woman and child gazing down at him.

The woman says, "I am your wife and this is your child." When he asks her why she has hands, the woman explains that her hands have grown back as a result of her travails and the deep care she received in the forest. The spirit brings the silver hands from a trunk in which they had been kept and shows them to the king. The king embraces his wife and child and after celebrating with the forest people, they return to their kingdom, where they are reunited with the old mother and have a second wedding.

In analyzing this tale, Clarissa Pinkola Estes suggests that in giving up her hands, a woman must look at the poor bargain she has made when she gives up her instinctive nature, her deep knowing, to please or protect the "father," the outer world point of view. In terms of the Heroine's Journey, a woman who has overidentified with the masculine culture has sacrificed something of great value to herself—her feeling and creative functions—which she must then journey inward to reclaim. In the act of losing her hands, she begins her initiation, which eventually leads to her individuation. As she wanders in the forest and regrows her hands, she moves from unconsciousness to consciousness. Our focus here will be her reconnection with the feminine.

After her wounding, the maiden begins her descent and is immediately assisted by a spiritual guide who helps her get food in the underworld. She eats the golden pears, shaped so much like a woman's womb, which represent the seed of the new self. We usually forget that the promise of the Descent is that it will nourish us even though it is dark and we feel that we have lost our way.[11]

In the garden the maiden meets three masculine allies: the gardener, the king, and the magician. Estes writes that the gardener represents "the regeneration of the maiden's soul, the king represents the ruling attitudes and laws in a woman's psyche, and the magician represents the direct magic of a woman's power—the instinctual feminine."[12]

There is a marriage between the king and the maiden, but the king must go on his own journey, so he leaves her in the company of his mother. Here the maiden comes into contact with the archetypal Mother energy. The king's mother watches over her while she is pregnant and is present when she gives birth. At some point, in order to protect her from the false messages being sent back and forth from the king, the mother has to send the maiden away to be initiated in the forest. She binds the infant to the maiden's breast so that she can nourish her child, and in the tradition of the old Goddess cults, she veils the maiden for her sacred pilgrimage.[13] The act of veiling allows the initiate to protect her new soul growth.

The maiden wanders into the forest and is met again by the spirit in white, another feminine presence who takes her into her home in the forest, where, over the next seven years, the maiden regrows her hands. The spirit in white guides the maiden and shelters her; in the same way, our instincts guide us to the next step of our journey. As we practice our deep instinctive knowing we, like the Handless Maiden, regrow our hands, "first as baby hands, then as the hands of a girl and finally, the hands of our womanhood."[14] If we do our own inner work, accept our own darkness and work toward consciousness, we will change, and the situation in which we find ourselves will change too. Our outer world will reflect our inner life; our deep listening will lead to wise choices.

The Handless Maiden is guided and protected by the archetypal feminine. In the following passage from Judith Duerk's *Circle of Stones,* we are asked to consider how our lives might be enriched if we each had access to a community of wise women to guide us on our journey:

> How might your life have been different, if there had been a place for you, a place of women? A place where other women, somewhat older, had reached out to help you as you rooted yourself in the earth of the ancient feminine. . . . A place where there was a deep understanding of the ways of woman to nurture you in every season of your life. A place of women to help you measure your own stature . . . to help you prepare and know when you were ready.
>
> A place where, after the fires were lighted, and the drumming, and the silence, you would claim, finally, in your Naming, as you spoke slowly into that silence, that the time had come, full circle, for you, also, to reach out . . . reach out as younger women entered into that place . . . reach out to help them prepare as they struck root in that same timeless earth. How might your life be different?

ART ACTIVITY: SPIRIT DOLLS

For most of us, the creative process resembles a quest. There is a gnawing sensation we carry deep within us that yearns for resolution. The activity of making spirit dolls helps us formulate the question that we carry in our hearts and points us toward possible answers. When I do Heroine's Journey workshops, my friend and co-teacher, Valerie T. Bechtol, asks participants to think about why they wish to make a spirit doll. She asks:

* What is your intention in bringing to life a spirit doll at this time in your journey?
* Why is this doll necessary?
* What do you need from her now?

Like the Handless Maiden, do you need a guide or ally to help you cross the threshold, to take the first step, to nurture you during your time in the underworld, to wait as fair witness while you undergo your transformation? Are you at a point in your life where you wish to ritualize the strengths you have developed along your journey, a spirit doll that symbolizes the wild and wise woman you have become? Are you looking for the archetypal Mother to hold you in your grief, confusion, or loneliness? Do you need to make a doll that reminds you of how to play?

The first step in creating your spirit doll is to gather materials. Once you decide that you're going to make a spirit doll, the materials will begin to present themselves to you. You may wish to make her body out of canvas, fabric, gauze, rusted metal, bones, shells, gourds, or cactus scabs. Her body can be made from sticks and bones and dressed with symbols and objects from nature or you may choose to make a soft body from canvas or fabric and stuff it with fiberfill. You can then paint it, cover it with mud, or sew objects on it.

Gather paints, brushes, glitter, sequins, feathers, buttons, glue, scissors, yarn, raffia, needles, and thread. Incorporate objects you find in nature as well as from your personal collection. Some women sew photographs or write poetry or journal entries directly on their doll; others hide prayers and intentions within the doll. The making of a spirit doll is a deeply personal ritual to bring to form a part of yourself that is emerging from your unconscious. Trust the process; let go of your preconceived notions of how your doll should look and assist the form it wishes to take.

Before you begin making your spirit doll, take five minutes or more and walk outside. Find a place, preferably in nature, where you can be by yourself and relax your mind and focus inward. Ask yourself the following questions:

* What do I need from my spirit doll?
* What color is she?
* What does she feel like?
* What does she smell like?
* What is her sound?
* What is my intention for birthing her at this time?[15]

Prepare a sacred space in which to make your doll. You may wish to burn sage, light a candle, play inspiring music. Give yourself at least two or three uninterrupted hours to begin your process. Let your doll evolve at her own pace.

Women in the Heroine's Journey workshops have made spirit dolls for many purposes: to spark and celebrate their creativity, to honor family members who have died, to deal with miscarriage or abortion, to celebrate the birth of the Wise Woman Within, and to represent the mothering and nurturance they never received. The following examples are from a workshop in New Mexico.

Janet never had a nurturing relationship with her mother, who was distant and critical and lacked a sense of connection to her feminine nature. Janet knew that she would never get the nourishment she needed from her mother, so she set out, in her late forties, to make conscious her own connection with the feminine. She decided to make a maternal spirit doll and gathered shells, beads, and feathers to use in creating a rather stylized doll.

To her surprise, when it was time to choose a fabric for the doll's body, she was drawn to an earthy brown color. This was a color she would not normally choose; she loved *bright* colors. At first, Janet was hesitant to use it, but she finally allowed herself to follow her intuition. She cut out a large female body shape, which she seamed and stuffed with cotton. What emerged was a doll with a soft but solid body with arms that joined together to embrace itself. Janet needed a symbol of the strong, nurturing feminine, and this large mothering form fit her need perfectly. She then covered the doll's body with mud in order to honor her connection to Mother Earth.

> *Without a well-built container, there can be no real psychological or spiritual development, because there is no safe place to put it.*
> —CAROL PEARSON

Elizabeth recently lost her eighteen-year-old son to an accidental drug overdose, and she was grieving deeply. In her grief, she had lost her voice and felt creatively blocked. She chose a cactus scab for the body of her spirit doll and wrote a letter to her son, which she incorporated into the body of the doll. She did a ritual of severance to release the pain and anger she felt about her son's death, and accepted Scabwoman to help carry her loss.

I had to make the difficult decision at age forty to have an abortion for health reasons. Because of what the medical establishment calls an "incompetent" cervix, and for several other reasons, the doctor did not think I would be able to carry to full term. Although my husband and I had made the decision together and had both grieved our loss in therapy and ritual, I did not feel complete with my grieving process until I made a spirit doll to honor the unborn fetus. One Christmas my friend Valerie gave me a box of red fabric, thread, yarn, and handmade paper and told me to make a doll. She knew that I was still dreaming six years later about the interrupted pregnancy.

I used a bent tree branch as the base for the doll's body so that she could lean forward giving birth, her arms wrapped together, holding her heart and chest in an embrace. As I enfolded red gauze and fabric around the wooden armature, I remembered a miscarriage I had had as a young woman and made a small bundle of babies to commemorate this loss as well. I put the doll on my altar and began to forgive myself for the fact that my body could not adequately maintain and nurture the pregnancy.

QUESTIONS FOR WRITING AND REFLECTION

Read through the following list of questions and pick the one that you wish to explore at present. Answer the remaining questions in depth in your own time frame.

* What is your sense of yourself as a woman at this time in your life? For instance, you might write something like one of the following: "I love being a woman and feel like I am in the full flower of expressing all parts of myself," or "I am just finding out what it means to me to be a woman outside of my roles of wife and mother," or "I am a woman in transition and uncertain about my future."
* How do you balance the different roles in your life? For instance, daughter, mother, career woman, friend, wife, lover?

* Are you comfortable expressing your feelings? Which feelings are you reluctant to express? Is your feeling style more like your mother's or father's?
* How do you express your love for your husband or wife?
* How do you express your love for your children or friends?
* How do you nurture your body? For instance, I take regular bubble baths, cook healthy meals, have massages (would love to have more manicures), and take long walks along the edge of the sea.
* How do you nurture your soul? For instance, you might set up an altar or focus of attention for meditation and prayer; do seasonal rituals; practice yoga, tai chi, or dance; take walks in the woods; or look at beautiful dawns or sunsets.
* How do you express your feminine nature? For instance, I am learning to trust my intuition, I love hugging my children, I am letting my hair grow, I am strengthening my body through yoga, I feel comfortable initiating lovemaking, I am relearning how to play piano, and I support Emily's List to elect more women.
* How do you express yourself creatively? For instance, you might express your creativity through art, music, dance, gardening, cooking, mothering, making love, mountain climbing, or arranging special objects in a place of beauty.
* What is your relationship to your sexuality? For instance, you might feel comfortable, active, indifferent, yearning, avoidant, scared, or confused. How does your comfort level with your sexuality reflect your first sexual experience?
* What is your relationship to the Earth, to nature, to gardening?

ART ACTIVITY: COLLAGE OF IMPORTANT WOMEN IN YOUR LIFE

Create a collage of the important women in your life, thinking about what you admire about them and how they inspire you. These women may be relatives, women from history, mythology, art, literature, politics, religion, film, and so on. Use magazine pictures, photographs, and old photos, which you might wish to photocopy and hand-color. Make a paper quilt or collage.

Dialogue with each woman as you add her to your collage. With each image, tell the woman why she has been selected and what it is about her that you wish to embody. How does the collage reflect aspects of yourself?

PERSONAL RITUALS

We create rituals to focus attention on and celebrate particular events in our lives, such as marriage, or to mark life cycles such as adolescence, midlife, and death. Some of the elements that are traditionally included in ritual are an invocation to Spirit; repetition of actions, sounds, songs, or words; a ritual object, such as a ring in marriage or the Torah scroll in the adolescence rites for a Jewish girl; movement or dance; and the willingness to enter into a nonordinary state.

In most rituals the elements of water, fire, air, and earth are utilized in some manner. For example, the lighting of candles frequently plays an important part in ritual, and the color of the candle reflects the occasion. Many women light black candles to celebrate midlife or menopause because black signifies the end of one cycle, that of giving birth to another, and entrance into another cycle, that of giving birth to the Wise Woman Within.

Rituals intensify our senses, break down our everyday masks, and usually involve the support and cohesiveness of a group to which we feel kinship. Some people create personal rituals to celebrate naming, friendship, pregnancy, giving birth, healing from illness, and the completion of academic, artistic, or athletic goals. Others create mourning rituals to honor miscarriage, divorce, descent, and death. Many parents create rituals to mark such transitions as a daughter's menstruation or a child's leaving home.

Create your own rituals to celebrate the transitions in your life. For example, prepare a personal ritual for your birthday, inviting only those people who honor you and have participated in your journey. Prepare a Wise Woman or Croning ritual for yourself as you celebrate your fiftieth year. Invite women who are both older and younger than you to share their wisdom.

The following is an example of some of the elements we included in a ritual to celebrate the fiftieth birthday of my friend Connie. We set up an altar with flowers and candles: a white candle to honor her as Maiden, a red candle to honor her as Mother, and a black candle to honor her as Crone. White celebrates a woman's virginity, the time during which she is one-in-herself. Red celebrates her blood and her ability to give birth. Black, which contains all color, celebrates the time of a woman's personal power. After an invocation calling upon the Great Mother to bless Connie and our circle, I said:

"Our culture does not honor aging, but we, as women, need to restore the honor and power of the Crone (Wise Woman) because we truly need her wisdom and whimsy. The Crone is the third aspect of the sacred feminine—Maiden, Mother, and Crone. The Maiden and Mother have been celebrated for centuries, but because most people in this culture fear a woman's power, the Crone is the missing link in the threefold aspect of the feminine. The Crone reminds us of our mortality; she is the one who tells us it is time to get on with it! She can get away with anything.

"Connie has invited us here today to celebrate her fiftieth birthday, marking her transition into her wisdom years. Although Connie has never needed our permission before to do exactly what she wants to do, now is the time in which she can truly get away with anything!

"Connie, the time of the Crone brings the harvest of your experience, when you reap the accumulated benefits of all that you have learned. As Crone:

You are the Wayshower, shining the light of wisdom for all of us to see.
You are the Windwoman, who knows the herbs and magic for healing.
You are the Dreamweaver, who presides in the dreamworld as our Guide.
You are the Goddess of the Crossroads, Hecate, intimate with the dark side of the moon, caves, dense forests, and all places of choice and change.
You are the Teacher, passing your knowledge on to the next generation.
You are the Celtic goddess Cerridwen, stirring your magical brew in the Cauldron of Inspiration.
You are the Seer whose skill in recalling the past guides you in divining the future.
You are the Transformer who brings renewal and continuation of all life.
You are the Knower of Mysteries, the secrets of existence, the magic of all things.
You are Mae West dripping sensuality from every pore of your body and shaking your tailfeather until the last day of your life!

"Connie, as you stand at the Crossroads stirring your Cauldron of Inspiration, we honor you as Wise Woman, Wayshower, Windwoman, Seer, Dreamweaver, Teacher, Knower of All Mysteries, and Mae West. You have traveled the path of Maiden and Mother, during which your life has focused on nurturing others. Now you begin the path of the Crone to nurture and birth your wisdom and creativity. Each of us will light your way with a black candle to celebrate your transformation."

At this point in the ritual, Connie named and honored each woman she had invited, from her college roommate, whom she had known the longest, to a new friend whom she had known for a relatively short time. She thanked each woman, in turn, for the part she had played in her life. The women ranged in age from seventy-two to her twenty-six-year-old daughter.

I then invited each woman to celebrate Connie by lighting her candle and offering her a gift of wisdom or whimsy. (Candles had been provided for each woman, and the request of a gift of wisdom or whimsy had been included in the invitation. As you can imagine, the gifts ranged from the hilarious to the sublime.) After each of us had bestowed our gifts and blessings, Connie asked that we take a moment to offer a silent blessing for ourselves and then blow out our candles. I closed the circle with gratitude to the Great Mother and Hecate for guidance and inspiration. We then feasted.

ARCHETYPAL DREAM IMAGES

We dream about images from our personal unconscious, which consists of experiences from childhood and our everyday life as well as more universal images, or what C. G. Jung called archetypes, such as the Great Mother or the Wise Old Man. These archetypal images are usually charged with intense energy. As many women today are searching for an experience of the divine feminine, they are having dreams, like the one at the beginning of this chapter, about a strong, nurturing woman who accompanies the dreamer as guide or companion. She often appears as a large, powerful, dark-skinned woman, a huge Black Goddess, who nurtures and creates life anew. Contemporary women also frequently report dreams of sisterly companions or a circle of women. They dream about ancient goddesses such as Artemis, goddess of the wilderness often represented by a deer; Athena, goddess of wisdom often represented by an owl; Hestia, goddess of the hearth; Aphrodite, goddess of love; Hecate, goddess of the crossroads; and the mother and daughter goddesses, Demeter and Persephone. Images of White Buffalo Woman or a Native American medicine woman; Kwan Yin, the goddess of compassion; and Kali, the goddess of death and destruction also appear repeatedly in many women's dreams. Menstrual dreams often contain the image of an otherworldly Lover, Intruder, or Unknown Man.

Images of animals figure prominently in women's dreams as well, particularly cats, horses, dogs, deer, snakes, and birds. "When an animal appears in a dream it brings an important message about our deep instinctual nature, the wisdom of our bodies, or our spontaneous feelings."[16] For example, a dream about a butterfly or frog, both animals that change forms, may indicate a time of transition and transformation. Not all animals are seen as helpful at first. When a dream image highlights a shadow side of yourself, a part you may deny, hide, or find repulsive, it may seem unsettling at first. Just try to receive the message the dream image brings.

RECORD THE DREAMS YOU HAVE WHILE WORKING WITH THIS CHAPTER.

5

Healing the
Mother-Daughter Split

> *There is a void felt these days by women and men—who suspect that*
> *their feminine nature, like Persephone, has gone to hell. Wherever*
> *there is such a void, such a gap or wound agape, healing must*
> *be sought in the blood of the wound itself. It is another of the old*
> *alchemical truths that "no solution should be made except in its*
> *own blood." So the female void cannot be cured by conjunction with*
> *the male, but rather by an internal conjunction, by an integration*
> *of its own parts, by a remembering or a putting back together of the*
> *mother-daughter body.*
> —NOR HALL, *The Moon and the Virgin*

The next stage of the Heroine's Journey involves healing the mother-daughter split, the initial separation from your feminine nature. For many women who have grown up in a patriarchal society, there has been a wounding that goes beyond a woman's relationship with her personal mother. It goes to the heart of the imbalance in values within our culture. We have buried our souls, our real feelings, our connection to our bodies and our imagination; we have separated from everything that makes life vital and creative. We are lonely for deep connection. We yearn for affiliation and community, for the positive, strong nurturing qualities of the feminine that have been missing from this culture.

If a woman has had a difficult relationship with her mother and recognizes how the feminine has been demeaned in our culture, she now has the challenge of bringing understanding and reconciliation to that relationship. Whether your personal mother was nurturing or cold, empowering or manipulative, present or absent, your internal relationship with her is integrated into your virtual psychological DNA as the mother complex. If your psyche integrated your mother in a negative or destructive way, you will feel split off from your positive feminine nature, and you'll have much work to do to reclaim it.

If your mother's attitudes threatened your very survival as a woman, you may have identified closely with the masculine, seeking salvation in it. Many women have found the spontaneous, fun-loving, nurturing aspect of the feminine within their fathers.

The nature of the mother-daughter split is also determined by how a woman integrates the archetypal Mother into her psyche, which includes Mother Earth, the Goddess, and the cultural view of the feminine. Our collective psyche fears the power of Mother and does everything it can to denigrate and destroy it. We take her nurturance for granted; we use, abuse, and dominate matter (*mater*) every time we get the chance. Our churches have pushed the feminine face of God underground for centuries, destroying her image and usurping her power for the male gods. How can we feel connected to the feminine when the culture around us does everything in its power to make us forget?

Healing the mother-daughter split involves grieving the initial separation from or rejection of your mother, as well as yourself, and then beginning to assimilate the feminine. The most important aspect of this stage is to grow an internal mother by becoming a nurturing mother to yourself.

It is a time to identify and reclaim feminine values for yourself:

* Honor your creativity.
* Live the values of your heart.
* Express the full spectrum of your emotions.
* Surround yourself with images that celebrate life.
* Speak with language that is inclusive.
* Honor your wisdom, compassion, and generativity and acknowledge the same in the other women in your life.
* Embrace women's power, which includes taking initiative, speaking out and leading others, and attaining power not for self-aggrandizement but for the good of others.

Women who have experienced a deep wounding in relationship to their personal mothers often seek their healing in the experience of the ordinary. For many, this takes the form of divine ordinariness: seeing the sacred in each and every ordinary act, whether it is washing the dishes, cleaning the toilet, or weeding the garden. Woman is nurtured and healed by grounding herself in the ordinary. Frequently during this period of reclaiming the inner feminine, you will find yourself immersed in learning about ancient goddesses to find the Wise Woman Within.

> *Each time you forget something, expand. Not only can this help you remember, but what happens is you get a delightful moment of peace when your mind blanks out, shuts up, is still.*
> —DAWNA MARKOVA

WOMAN AS MYTHMAKER

Mythmaking is an ongoing process, and myths are necessary to organize life. If a woman has not been initiated into a feminine mythology by her mother or grandmother, she has to develop her own relationship to her inner feminine, to the Great Mother. This may explain why so many women today seek ancient images of powerful feminine deities and heroines to heal the wound within. Because female history has been so shattered, women are reaching back to prehistory to find elements of woman's mythology that existed before the Greek division of power into multiple gods.

As archeologists uncover ancient cultures based on the life-giving principles of the Goddess, women reclaim the power and dignity once accorded to them when the role of woman was to protect human life and the sacredness of nature. The vision and power of the feminine is represented in depictions of the Virgin, Mother, and Crone; the spider, snake, and bird; the vessel, cave, and grail; the mountain, water, and trees; as well as in specific cultural goddess figures such as Isis, Sophia, Demeter, Inanna, Kali, Cerridwen, Lilith, Coatlicue, Kwan Yin, Yemaya, Amaterasu, and many, many more. These representations capture the essence of the feminine aspects of creatrix, preserver, and destroyer and celebrate the preservation of, reverence for, and interconnection of the basic elements of life.[1]

> *As I go into her, she pierces my heart. As I penetrate further, she unveils me. When I have reached her center, I am weeping openly. I have known her all my life, yet she reveals stories to me, and these stories are revelations and I am transformed.*
> —SUSAN GRIFFIN

Women today are dreaming about strong, nurturing women who have no need to dominate others to exhibit power but who come to the dreamer to wake her up to a new order.

They dream of the dark, of the need to face the harsh realities of life and death, of the possibility of cataclysm, suffering, and psychosis. Many dreamers encounter a large, powerful, dark-skinned woman who nurtures them and creates them anew. The poet May Sarton describes her to us in "The Invocation to Kali":

Kali, be with us.
Violence, destruction, receive our homage.
Help us to bring darkness into the light,
To lift out the pain, the anger,
Where it can be seen for what it is—
The balance-wheel for our vulnerable, aching love.
Put the wild hunger where it belongs,
Within the act of creation,
Crude power that forges a balance
Between hate and love.

Help us to be the always hopeful,
Gardeners of the spirit
Who know that without darkness
Nothing comes to birth
As without light
Nothing flowers.

Bear the roots in mind,
You, the dark one, Kali,
Awesome power.[2]

TAKING BACK THE DARK: RECLAIMING THE MADWOMAN

In *Kiss Sleeping Beauty Good-bye,* Madonna Kolbenschlag urges us to reverse the pattern of fairy tales, to go back and restore and heal the female constellations that have for so long carried the evil element in the story. It is imperative that we reclaim and reintegrate the repressed parts of the feminine that are embodied as witches, evil stepmothers, and madwomen. Stepmothers, witches, and madwomen are characteristically portrayed as women who present obstacles to the developing girl child. They are described as mean, cruel, withholding, manipulative, jealous, and greedy. Their wicked deeds are usually punished by death. The witch is pushed into an oven in "Hansel and Gretel"; the stepmother in "Snow White and the Seven Dwarfs" dances to her death in slippers that have been heated over hot coals; and the Wicked Witch of the West melts in *The Wizard of Oz*.

In the fairy tale there is little concern for the origins of cruelty in the stepmother or wicked witch; we just assume that she was always that way. The wicked stepmother represents the disappointment each child carries at not having the "perfect" mother, that illusory mother-next-door who is ever-present, ever-understanding, and unconditionally loving (and never harried and short-tempered coming home from a long, difficult day at work!).

There is a folktale, however, in which a daughter opens the door and takes back her mother. In doing so, she heals those repressed parts of the feminine that most of us choose not to see and refuse to accept and understand. This is the work of healing the Mother-Daughter split.

Once upon a time there lived a woman with four daughters. She loved her daughters one, two, and three, who were clever, fair, and beautiful, but hated her youngest, Mesmeranda, who was Just Who She Was. Each day she went out to gather food for her children. As she returned, her daughters would hear her sing:

> My darling daughters,
> One, two, and three,
> Come to Mama, come to me.
> Mesmeranda, daughter four,
> Stay behind the kitchen door.

The girls ran to the door to let their mother in, but Mesmeranda stayed behind the kitchen door yearning to be a part of the family. Then the mother prepared dinner for the three older daughters, and as they ate together, talking and laughing, they threw the leftovers to Mesmeranda. The older girls grew and prospered and Mesmeranda remained thin and frail.

Now there lurked outside a wolf who watched the mother's comings and goings and hungered for her three plump daughters. He thought he could catch them by singing the mother's song. He practiced for days and nights, and one afternoon while she was away, he went to the door and sang:

My darling daughters,
One, two, and three,
Come to Mama, come to me.
Mesmeranda, daughter four,
Stay behind the kitchen door.

Nothing happened. The girls did not open the door because the voice of the wolf was low and gruff. Foiled, the wolf went off to see Coyote. "I need a mother's voice," he said. "Make my voice sound high and sweet." Coyote looked at the wolf. "What will you give me in return?" he asked. "One of the mother's daughters," replied the wolf. Coyote tuned the wolf's voice, and the wolf returned to the house of the daughters and sang:

My darling daughters,
One, two, and three,
Come to Mama, come to me.
Mesmeranda, daughter four,
Stay behind the kitchen door.

This time the wolf's voice was so high it flew on the wind. The girls laughed and said to each other, "Oh, that's just the leaves whispering," and did not open the door. Some time later the mother returned and sang her song to her daughters. At once they opened the door, and again the four ate, leaving the leftovers for Mesmeranda.

The next day the wolf returned to Coyote and complained. "You made my voice too thin. Fix it so I sound like a woman." Coyote cast a spell on the wolf, and the wolf returned to the house of the daughters. This time he sang just like the mother:

My darling daughters,
One, two, and three,

Come to Mama, come to me.
Mesmeranda, daughter four,
Stay behind the kitchen door.

The girls ran to greet their mother, and the wolf stuffed them into a sack and carried them off. Mesmeranda remained behind the kitchen door. Later that day the mother returned and sang at the door:

My darling daughters
One, two, and three,
Come to Mama, come to me.
Mesmeranda, daughter four,
Stay behind the kitchen door.

No one came to the door, so she sang her song again. Again no one came, and she began to fear the worst. Then she heard a faint voice singing.

Mama, your daughters,
One, two, and three,
Can no longer hear, can no longer see.
They've gone away and are no longer free.
Mesmeranda is here, look at me.

The mother threw open the door, and when she did not see her beloved daughters, she ran from the house like a madwoman, pulling at her hair and singing her song over and over.

Mesmeranda stood up, saw the empty room, and walked out the open door. She began her journey, made her way in the world, and eventually married the emperor's son. Time passed.

One day an old madwoman, whose hair was wild and tangled like a hornet's nest, was heard singing at the palace gate:

My darling daughters,
One, two, and three,

Can no longer hear, can no longer see.
Mesmeranda, daughter four,
Hear me now, I'm at your door.

People laughed as they passed her by, and the palace guards told her to move on. But each day she returned in her tattered rags and sang:

My darling daughters,
One, two, and three,
Can no longer hear, can no longer see.
Mesmeranda, daughter four,
Hear me now, I'm at your door.

Word reached the empress that there was a madwoman in the streets singing for her daughter Mesmeranda. Mesmeranda said, "I know no madwoman and I have no mother."

One day Mesmeranda was pulling weeds and planting vegetables in the palace garden and heard her name in the madwoman's refrain. She opened the gate and looked into the face of the madwoman. There she saw her mother. She took her hand and brought her in.

"Mama," she said, "the others are gone. But look at me. I am Mesmeranda. You did not love me before and I stayed behind the kitchen door. But now I am here and I will take care of you." Then she bathed her mother, dressed her, and brushed out her hair.[3]

Mesmeranda welcomes her mother, cleanses her, clothes her, and cares for her. She opens up her heart and takes back the Madwoman who was the mother who rejected her. Each one of us has to take back the discarded feminine in order to reclaim our full feminine power. If a woman continues to resent her mother for the lack of mothering she received, she remains bound to this woman, a perennial daughter-in-waiting. She refuses to grow up, although to the outside world she appears to function as a mature adult. In her depths, she feels unworthy and incomplete. In her book by the same name, Marion Woodman names this outcast part of a woman the "pregnant virgin"—the part who comes to consciousness through going into the darkness, mining her leaden darkness, until she brings her silver out.[4]

Over the years I have found it difficult to accept and cherish the madwoman within my mother because then I will have to face the madwoman within myself. It's so much easier to project my disowned parts (like rage and powerlessness) onto my mother, who has carried so many of my unfulfilled expectations. I have come to accept that taking back my mother the way she is means that I will never be able to make her love me the way I want to be loved. I will never have a mommy who openly loves: a mother, yes, but not a mommy.

This process of slowly accepting my mother as she is has been the result of doing repeated rituals of healing the mother-daughter split, which is a gentle way of working consciously with this wound. (The ritual is included in this chapter.) Marion Woodman writes, "To reach the place where we belong to ourselves, we have to sever the umbilical cord that binds us to archaic dependencies. If we have never known a loving mother, that severing can be even more difficult, because we continue to long for what we have never had. We continue to seek Mother in our relationships."[5]

TASKS IN HEALING YOUR FEMININE NATURE

Wise women have natural immunity. They let everything ebb and flow, without work, without desiring. They let go of expectations and they are never at a loss. Because they are not at a loss, their spirits live forever.
—PAMELA METZ AND JACQUELINE TOBIN, *The Tao of Women*

If you never experienced comfort from your mother, you probably have a difficult time finding deep soul comfort within your relationships. It is unfamiliar. Your task is to create that sense of soul comfort within yourself.

If you never experienced compassion from your mother, you probably have little patience with your own human failings as well as those of others. Your task is to observe someone who practices compassion and to practice it yourself.

If your mother stifled your creativity, your task is to give voice to each creative impulse that presents itself. Paint, write poetry, drum, garden, cook, and dance!

If your mother despised or rejected her own body as a woman, your task is to embrace and honor your body and your sexuality.

If you felt abandoned by your mother for whatever reason, including depression or alcoholism, your task will be to listen to your feelings and never abandon yourself.

If you have some unfinished business with your mother and she has died or is emotionally unavailable, you can write her a letter (which you keep or send to yourself) expressing your grief or anger about the loss of a nurturing mother, or tell her how you have come to understand and accept her as she is. You may then be able to feel gratitude for her presence in your life.

Each one of us carries our mother forward, so it is necessary to heal the mother-daughter split whether your mother is alive or not, in order to heal the deep wounding of your feminine nature. The key element here is to become a good mother to yourself. With that in mind, take on the task of mothering yourself.

I know that for myself, a father's daughter with an emotionally rejecting mother, I continued to look for the mothering I hadn't received from her by seeking the attention and approval of older female mentors, such as Polly McVickar and Dr. Jean Houston, throughout my twenties and thirties. I also continued to reach out to my mother for understanding and acceptance. Sometime in my early forties, I came to terms with the fact that I would never have the type of guidance and love that I longed for from my mother. Although I continued to develop friendships with women who were mothering, I mourned the loss of the dream I yearned for, accepted the loss, and let it go. When you stop seeking healing from a source outside yourself, you can:

* Begin to cultivate your own unique feminine sensibility by making space to listen to your feelings and respond to them.
* Listen to your body and respect its limits.
* Listen to your intuition; don't override it.
* Listen to the voice of your creativity and respect each aspect of yourself that wants to be expressed at this time.
* Attend to your safety and make nurturing decisions for yourself.

At the same time you are developing a response to your inner life, you can take steps in the outer world by doing the following:

* Actualize your dreams. For example, if you have a dream of becoming a writer, take a writing course, schedule weekly or daily uninterrupted writing time, and write! If you want to change careers, research alternatives in the library or on the web, or invest in yourself by going to a career counselor.
* Put your hands in the earth: garden, have a massage, bake bread, watch the cycles of nature and become aware of your own rhythms in relationship to seasonal cycles.
* Cultivate and support your women friends.
* Join a woman's group; healing occurs within the female matrix.
* Go to a library or bookstore and take out books to research the sacred feminine.
* Participate in the nurturing of your community.

RITUAL: HEALING THE MOTHER-DAUGHTER SPLIT

The focus of this ritual is to heal the relationship between you and your mother (or you and your daughter). This ritual can be done alone or with a group of women who are also committed to healing their mother-daughter split. If you are not in a women's group, ask for the support and presence of a close woman friend. In choosing to do this ritual, you not only set the intention of healing your relationship with your mother but also invite yourself to align with what is needed to heal the split within your feminine nature.

Create a beautiful altar with flowers, a candle, and an image or statue of the Goddess to honor your relationship with your mother. Select a photograph of your mother or an object she has given you, which you will place on the altar later during the ritual. As you begin your ritual, call upon the guidance and wisdom of the Mother God.

Whether you felt loved by your mother, accepted, protected, nurtured, and cherished, or rejected, abandoned, and criticized; whether your mother was present or absent, able to

When my mother asked me if I had become a woman yet, I did not understand. I thought she meant in age, not in that way. And summer after summer she would ask me the same question, and each time she looked more worried. I did not pay much attention to her.

—VELMA WALLIS

touch you or not; in this ritual you have chosen to honor your mother in order to come to some acceptance of who she is or was in your life.

At some level your mother did the best she could in relation to her particular family background, the historical period in which she lived, her own mothering or lack of it, her health, economic status, and marital status, what was permitted for her as a woman in the collective, and the support she received for her mothering from a spouse or from the culture.

Honor her strength, wisdom, and understanding, and offer gratitude to her for choosing to birth you. You may not actually feel this, but the point here is to create an open heart so that you can believe your mother did the best she could. In doing this ritual, you heal your mother's wounds as well as your own, so that you no longer have to carry your mother's pain but can begin to carry her light.

Think about what it is that you need in this ritual in relationship to your mother. For example, do you need to understand her, forgive her, call her accountable, accept her, reclaim some aspect of her that she has hidden, mourn her, let her go, ask her to let go of you?

Place your object or photograph on the altar and speak your womanline aloud. For example, I would say, "I am Maureen Elizabeth, granddaughter of Julia Frances Virginia Dunn, daughter of Julia Frances Virginia, sister of Rosemary Teresa, mother of Heather and Brendan."

If you participate in this ritual with others, tell a reminiscence about your mother. Then talk directly to your mother and tell her what you appreciate about her or what you still need from her. When you are finished, light a candle for your mother, bless her, and let her go.

The following examples are from a group ritual that was part of a weekend Heroine's Journey workshop in the Pacific Northwest.

Ellen called her mother in the middle of the night two days before our workshop ritual in order to borrow her locket. She put it on the altar with a smile and told us this was her favorite piece of her mother's jewelry because it carried a secret. Inside the locket was a photograph of her father, and underneath that was a photograph of another man, named "Cowboy Mike," who had been in her mother's life before her father. Ellen said the locket represented a spark her mother carried hidden within herself. Ellen wanted to reclaim this spark for herself. When she spoke to her mother in ritual, she asked her for a spark of spunk for herself!

Francine placed a photograph on the altar of a beautiful woman coiffed in vintage forties style and said, "My mother was a heavy smoker and addicted to barbiturates. She died because she did not know how to take care of herself. She taught her children how to care for themselves, but she couldn't do the same for herself. She died of emphysema and liver failure.

"She was a strong woman, an army nurse during the Second World War. She delivered me herself and cut my umbilical cord with her sewing scissors. She had called the hospital to come and get her, but they didn't believe she could be delivering so fast. After she delivered me, she called them back and held the phone to the sound of the wailing baby who was me and said, 'Now do you believe me?' They sent an ambulance."

Francine then said, "I want to honor my mother for her strength, but I wish she had gotten help for her problems. I hold her accountable for being an addict. She died when I was very young and I missed having her as my mother."

Ginny put a spiny seashell on the altar and said, "My mother never went to AA, so I cannot call her an alcoholic but she had a drinking problem. She sent me this shell from Florida after she had visited me and noticed that I collected rocks and shells. This shell represents her; it is hard and brittle on the surface just like my mother. She was cold and cruel to me as a child and held me at a distance. The inside of this shell is pink, delicate, and beautiful. I know that my mother must be a beautiful person inside, because the people in her church community value her. She just never showed that side of herself to me.

"My mother never learned how to value herself living with my father, who was bigger than life. My tears are for her inability to express her feelings in any other way but rage. She did not have the support from women like we have now. She might have been a different person if she had."

GUIDED IMAGERY: WOMANLINE

Do this exercise, if possible, to the sound of a drumbeat or in silence.

In this exercise you will be walking backward in time along your womanline. Your womanline is the thread that connects you to the female ancestors in your family: your mother, grandmother, great-grandmother, and so forth. The purpose of this exercise is to identify the strengths and gifts of each woman and claim them as part of their legacy to you.

Stand, close your eyes, and focus your attention on your breath. Be aware of your body and your connection to the earth. Take three deep breaths. (Pause.) With each exhalation your body becomes more and more relaxed and you move into deeper and deeper levels of consciousness, where more images are accessible to you. Now imagine, if you will, that you are standing in the middle of a very beautiful meadow. You notice the environment around you, the colors, textures, smells, and sounds.

Now take a step backward and step into the shoes of your mother. (Pause.) As you step into your mother's shoes, become aware of her environment. Where does she live? Notice the colors, smells, sounds, and textures. What foods does your mother love? Feel her emotions, her dreams, her aspirations. Feel her longings, her frustrations. Become aware of her strengths and skills. What does she know about being a woman? How has she empowered herself as a woman? (Stay with the image as long as it feels alive.)

Now, take a step backward and step into the shoes of your grandmother. As you step into your grandmother's shoes, notice her environment. What are the colors, sounds, smells, and textures in her life?' What foods does she prepare? Feel her body, her emotions, her dreams, her aspirations. What are her special strengths and skills? How does she celebrate life? What does she know about being a woman? (Pause several minutes.)

Now, once again, take a step backward in time, and step into the shoes of your great-grandmother. Although you probably never knew her or even heard stories about her, draw upon your imagination. Notice the times and culture in which she lives. What are the colors, textures, and sounds in her environment? What are the smells? What does she cook? Become aware of the people in her life. Feel her body, her emotions, her dreams, her aspirations. Feel her longings, her frustrations. What are her strengths and skills? What does she know about being a woman? (Pause.)

Now, take a step back along your womanline to two hundred years ago and stand in the shoes of your ancestor at that time. Using your imagination, look around. What country does she live in? What is her dwelling like? Does she live in the country or the city? What race is she? What is her physical appearance? What clothes does she wear? What foods does she cook? Does she have children? Is she married? What are the activities of her daily life? Feel her physical strength and stamina. Become aware of her emotions, her dreams, her aspirations. What does her life teach you about being a woman? (Stay with the image as long as it feels alive.)

Now, take another step back in time along your womanline to five hundred years ago, to the Middle Ages. What country does your ancestor live in? Stand in the shoes of your ancestor and become aware of her environment. Notice the colors, sounds, smells, textures, tastes. What foods does she like? What are the activities of her daily life? Who are the people in her life? What does she like to do? Notice her skills and talents. Feel her physical strength and stamina. What does her life teach you about being a woman? (Pause.)

Now, take a step back in time to five thousand years ago, to a time when the Goddess was revered. You find yourself in a clearing surrounded by trees. Your Goddess ancestor steps forward to greet you. Notice how she is dressed; notice her presence.

She takes your hands and leads you to her home, where you are the honored guest. You absorb the colors, textures, sounds, and smells of her environment. She feeds you finger foods and gives you a drink to celebrate your journey. She shows you her handicrafts and instructs you in the skills of her crafts and the herbs of her healing. She shows you how she lives and asks you about your life. She shares her creativity, wisdom, and rituals with you. She teaches you about honoring the sacred feminine. (Stay with the image as long as it feels alive.)

Before you take your leave, your Goddess ancestor takes your hands, looks deeply into your eyes, and gives you a gift. (The gift may be an object, a symbol, a word, a song, a dance, etc.) She tells you to bring the gift to the women of your womanline and to remind them never to forget who they are.

With gratitude, you take your leave and step forward.

Gently move forward now in time along your womanline to the ancestor of five hundred years ago. She awaits you and reaches out to take your hands. You feel her hands, the joys, sorrows, and love they hold. You honor her and tell her about your ancient Goddess ancestor. You show her the gift she gave to you. She tells you that because of your journey she is healed in some particular way. She gives you her blessing and a gift to bring forward on your journey. (Pause.) You accept the gift, embrace her, and leave. Now, take a step forward.

Continue walking forward on your womanline, greeting each one of your ancestors—including your great-grandmother and grandmother—until you reach your mother. Along the way, tell each ancestor about the women who have come before her. Share and exchange the gifts and skills given to you to bring forward to the women of today. Each woman recognizes the healing power of your journey and thanks you.

Now walk forward in time along your womanline to the time of your mother. She awaits you and reaches out to take your hands. You feel her hands, the joys, sorrows, and love they hold. You honor her and tell her about your ancient ancestors. She tells you that because of your journey she is healed in some particular way. She teaches you a skill or gives you a gift of her creativity to take forward on your journey. (Pause.) You accept it, embrace her, and leave. You take a step forward.

Walk forward now and find yourself once again in the meadow where you first began your journey. Become aware of your feet upon the earth and feel the strength of your body. You are empowered by all of the women of your womanline—their health, gifts, creativity, wisdom. Hold the gifts given to you by your ancestors and reach forward in time and give them to your daughter or the women who will follow after you. (Pause.) Know that you carry the wisdom and creativity of all these women within you. Become aware of your physical body and start to bring yourself back to full waking consciousness. Take a deep breath, count to five, and open your eyes. Express your experience through writing, poetry, paint, dance, clay, collage, spoken word, or song.

The following poem by Tina Michelle Datsko was written during a Heroine's Journey workshop.

MOMMA AND THE DEATH BOUTIQUE
1.
The glass door closes behind me,
and I am swallowed by the cryogenic cool
of air conditioning. Florescent
lights buzz perniciously overhead.
The salon's interior is entirely typical.
Glass shelves extol a European mystique,
whispering a creamy transcendence of mortality.
I am looking for my mother.
I speak to the counter girl.

Are my lips moving? I can't hear any sound.
Her wide dark Puerto Rican eyes shine
blankly back at me. She smiles
prettily and from between her shell
white teeth comes music. Rising, falling,
burbling, a stream in a dark wood.
I push past to the inner sanctum.
It is even colder here and dim.
The hunching room is broken
into cubicles. I rove, thrashing
back the curtains till I find
her. She is slabbed out on a slick
polyurethane upholstered aesthetician's
recliner. Garbed in a blue paper gown,
paper hair net, paper booties.
She looks relaxed and pampered.
I scream.
Then I plead as the pretty young girl
poises the needle for annihilation.
"No, Momma, No! Don't go! I'm not
ready for you to go!"
She looks at me coldly. Her hooked fish
mouth presses tighter.
The needle stings her blue-blooded alabaster arm.
I scream and sob myself awake.
My lover enfolds me to his heart
and my horror hyperventilates me.
In our boxcar apartment
in the Calle Convento
in Santurce, humid night bathes
me. *Coqui. Coqui. Coqui.*

2.
Last night, hovering in the amniotic bath
I was cleansed. Guilt vortexed

down that drain.
Momma, you shut the piano, blackened
its smile, and chose to vanish.
Momma, I cannot lay down
my pen, surrender. You made me
stronger than you. Every breath you
took from me came back to me doubled.
The words I buried never died.
They have grown now into a great tree
spreading above and below
with ripe pears ready for the picking.[6]

DREAM RITUALS

You may wish to use a ritual as a way of physically depicting an inner attitude change that a dream calls for. The best rituals are physical, solitary, and silent. Approach your ritual with consciousness and reverence.

Years ago I had a dream about root vegetables that were jammed into one small clay pot, strangling because of lack of air and space. In the dream I carefully separated them and put them into their own pots. At the time of the dream, my twenty-seven-year-old son and I were involved in a separation process that was painful to us both. Each of us was acting out the hurt and rejection we felt because of our long-time enmeshment.

> *Detachment liberates the heart from the past and from the future. It gives us the freedom to be who we are, loving others for who they are.*
> —MARION WOODMAN

After having the dream, I decided to photograph root vegetables, both together and apart. For several weeks I collected vegetables with the most tangled roots at the local farmers' market and photographed them against a black velvet background. As I made the prints and looked at both the individual and the paired vegetables, I realized I was ritualizing the dream. It was certainly time for me to extricate my roots from my son's and to let him "breathe" in his own container. Several months later, he prepared to move three thousand miles from home.

Sara, a thirty-five-year-old woman in my women's dream group, had a dream about a beautiful, full-length red wool cape that represented her femininity. She had been grieving the stillbirth of her baby a year previous to the dream and knew that the cape represented an emerging aspect of her healed feminine nature. When the other women in the group suggested that she ritualize the dream, she went right out and bought a pattern and red cashmere wool fabric to make the cape.

RECORD THE DREAMS YOU HAVE WHILE WORKING WITH THIS CHAPTER.

6

Healing the Wounded Masculine

*To cut off the head of the patriarchy within us is to cut off the power
drives—the injunctions, the rules, false reasonings, false values that
separate us from our reality and take our voice away.*
—MARION WOODMAN AND ELINOR DICKSON, *Dancing in the Flames*

In the legend of the Holy Grail, Parsifal searched for the Grail, the chalice
used by Christ at the Last Supper and the ancient cauldron of the Great Goddess. Parsifal ventured into the Grail Castle, where he saw the Fisher King,
who had a wound in his genitals or thigh, a wound that would not heal. The
Grail itself could heal him; a young innocent fool such as Parsifal was needed
to see that something was wrong, to have compassion, and to ask, "What ails
thee?" Only then would the healing qualities of the Grail become available to
the king. But Parsifal could not ask the question because when he first ventured into the Grail Castle, he had not yet done the difficult work of coming
to consciousness.

The king represents the ruling principle in our psyches and in the culture.
He blesses, encourages creativity, and establishes an ordered universe by his
presence alone. The wound in the thigh means that the king is wounded in his
generative ability, his capacity for relationship. Like the Fisher King, we, too,
are wounded in our ability to relate to our deep inner self, our feminine capacity
for growth and creation. And like Parsifal, whose name means "He who draws
the opposites together," we are blind to the fact that we are out of balance. Until
an aspect of ourselves recognizes our pain, has compassion, and asks, "What
ails thee?" we will not be healed.

We are split off from a relationship with our creative feminine; our rational mind devalues and ignores it as we refuse to listen to our intuition, our feelings, the deep wisdom of our body. We feel the sadness and loneliness of alienation, yet we do not recognize that these feelings result from an imbalance within our nature.

> *The questioning itself suffices because it is the speaking, the true soul gesture of an act of compassion, that heals.*
> —ROBERT SARDELLO

The masculine is an archetypal force; it is not a gender. Like the feminine, it is a creative force that lives within all women and men. In its positive aspect, it is protective, outer-directed, rational, ordered, and supportive. It serves as the bridge from our creative imagination and dreams to the actualization of them. When it becomes unbalanced and unrelated to life, it becomes combative, judgmental, and destructive. This unrelated archetypal masculine can be cold, distant, and inhuman; it does not take into account our human limitations. It demands perfection, control, and domination; nothing is ever enough. Many of us are like the Fisher King—our masculine nature is wounded.

The Grail is the symbol of the sacred, creative feminine principle, which is accessible to us all. The Grail can heal the king just as the feminine can heal our masculine nature. In the legend, the Grail was carried at all times by the Grail Maiden, but Parsifal and the king did not see it.

Parsifal had the experience of the Grail, the Grail Castle, and the wounded Fisher King, but he did not ask, "What ails thee?" If we are to heal, we must make this question conscious. The unrelated, out-of-control, masculine element within each one of us drives us beyond a point of balance. I had the experience of being at the mercy of my own perfectionist masculine nature in trying to finish my book *Fathers' Daughters* on deadline. I let my unrelenting "driver" take over, worked maniacally around the clock to send my manuscript in to my publisher on time, and had a full collapse. I succeeded in satisfying my inner tyrant at great expense to my physical and emotional health.

In healing the wounded masculine, we have to identify the qualities of the wounded masculine within ourselves that we have projected onto the men in our lives. Unless these unconscious parts of our psyche are brought to some level of awareness, we "see" these traits and characteristics in other people in our lives and feel either attracted to or repelled by them. This is what is known as projection of our shadow. Whether our husbands, lovers, sons, fathers, and male colleagues actually embody such qualities as rigidity, criticism, disconnection from feelings, blind ambition, and desire for control or not, they shoulder these and other disowned parts of ourselves.

At times, the men in our lives also carry the unexpressed parts of our positive masculine nature. A client of mine has recently separated from her partner of sixteen years. Although Carol is financially self-sufficient as a business consultant, she relied on Hank to fill the role of protector and to carry the illusion of provider. If anything went wrong with her car or in their home, she would call Hank. He loved to solve problems and was identified with his role of fixer. Although Carol is extremely competent at work, she does not know how to change a fuse or locate a plumber in whom she would feel confident. Hank always took care of these tasks, and Carol could always count on him.

> *The system is always going to collapse until you're on course.*
> —CAROLYN MYSE

It is true that in most relationships there is a division of labor and responsibility, but like Carol, some women feel powerless to assume the more "masculine-oriented" skills usually assumed by their partners, male or female. She says, "I've never thought of myself as a dependent woman, and it is very hard admitting just how much I relied on Hank to take care of me."

In identifying the wounded masculine, we have to look at the parts of ourselves that have been repressive to our bodies, have abandoned our feelings, or have aggressively denied and overridden our limits, intuition, and dreams. We need to recognize our inner annihilating critic, who demands perfection and reminds us that what we do is never good enough, as well as the persistent driver that never lets us stop. We have to examine the parts of ourselves that are adversarial, domineering, power hungry, rigid, jealous, acquisitive, and relentlessly competitive.

At a time when 50+ percent of American women are the sole or primary breadwinners for their families, earning at least half of their family's income, it is important that women integrate strong positive masculine traits. But it is also important that we remember who we are as *women*. We can do that by developing a strong belief in ourselves, the ability to follow through and back ourselves up, the vision to examine all possibilities, the courage to grow an internal toughness and stand our ground, the willingness to make mistakes, and a healthy competitiveness. We must grow a strong internal Protector,

> *Women often need to go back to the Ego archetypes and shore up their Ego strength before they can manifest true Selves and their gifts in the world. Unless women do so, they may find their true Souls but be unable to bring back the wisdom they gained on their inner journeys to benefit the world.*
> —CAROL PEARSON

build a healthy bridge between our images and the manifestation of them, and develop an internal supportive masculine guide, a man with heart. We must claim our own authority by speaking our truth as *women* and by sharing our feminine wisdom with others.

MASCULINE DREAM FIGURES

It is often difficult to identify something as vague as the masculine aspect of ourselves until we look at the qualities of the male characters in our dreams. These inner male figures carry our masculine qualities and often serve as invaluable guides. In the following two dreams, the dreamer, Antonia, cultivates a relationship with her inner positive masculine nature, embodied first by a craftsman and then by a fisherman.

> I am in an old "hacienda." It is a very large property and it seems quite ancient. There are stone courtyards with fountains and very old bougainvillea vines twisting up the walls. Everything seems very quiet and solitary, as if the place has been abandoned. I walk around to the back and enter a workshop where I see the craftsman working with his back to me. He is welding and sculpting something over blue and yellow flames. I hear him singing out the properties of the materials he is working with, like an alchemical incantation. As I listen closely, I realize that he is singing about me. "She was born in the year of the Dragon, a water dragon." He goes on to name and sing out characteristics that are specific to me. As I watch him work, I suddenly realize that this is the workshop where relationships are crafted, relationships that will later manifest in the external world, and he is creating one for me. I am delighted and curious. As I approach, it is clear to me that I may watch and listen but not speak or interfere with the process in any way. The craftsman stands back to look at his work every so often, and he is obviously delighted with the result. I hear him say, "This one is a real work of art—he'll never know what hit him."

The masculine figure in the dream is active. He combines metal elements with the fire of transformation to create something new for the dreamer. It is clear that he cares deeply for her, knows her well enough to enumerate her qualities, and is preparing something of great value for her. He is a positive guide.

The dreamer has great respect for what the craftsman is making. She knows that he is crafting a relationship in the external world that will complement who she is. She also knows not to interfere with the process; she must wait and hold the tension of not knowing. What is to manifest in the outer world is carefully being forged in the fires of her unconscious. What she brings to the alchemical process is an aware presence, which she has developed over the years through her meditation practice.

Waiting and holding the tension of not knowing is a discipline that is part of the creative process. When something new is coming into being, there is a period of gathering ideas, sorting material, and listening to our dreams and intuition. During this time it feels as if nothing is happening, and it is important not to allow the critic to interfere. If we bring the critic into the process too soon, we eliminate the possibility of living with the unknown. Although the unknown creates enormous anxiety, which most of us resist at any cost, it is the place of great fertility and growth. We just have to endure it.

Nine months (the symbol of pregnancy) after having this dream, the dreamer became conscious of feeling continually distanced in her relationship with her lover. She never felt that he was making a "clear choice" to be in relationship with her, and she concluded that he would never make a long-term commitment. Although she loved him deeply, she did a ritual of severance in which she let go of her "attachment to the unavailable man" to make room for a partner who was not afraid to love her completely. A week later she broke off the relationship knowing that she could no longer compromise her own nature by settling for a situation in which she was not a clear choice. She said, "I can't expect someone else to make me a conscious choice until I make a clear choice to be in relationship with myself." After this, she became aware of a strong inner presence who said, "She is my beloved." Within a month she had the following dream:

> I see a strong, simple fisherman, skillfully mending his nets, sitting alone in a room by the edge of the sea. He is concentrating on his work and seems very intent and very humble. I come into the room with a feeling of having covered long distances and examined many choices. I tell him that after seeing all I have seen and traveling to all the places

I have been, I have chosen to be with him. He looks up from his work, his eyes very bright, his face shining. He can hardly believe that I have actually chosen him and he is overjoyed.

In this dream, the feminine figure, Antonia, is active; she makes a conscious choice to love the fisherman. This decision has been a long time coming; she has made her journey, has done her inner work, and has examined many options before choosing a relationship with a man who knows about the depths. This time the masculine figure in the dream is the one who allows the process to unfold. While he waits, he sits alone and goes about his everyday tasks—mending nets after catching fish. The fisherman and the act of catching fish are often symbolic of the Christ consciousness. The dreamer has chosen to be in relationship with her own divine masculine nature. She has made a commitment to herself.

Within four months Antonia quit her job as a translator for a large corporation. She had not been dissatisfied with her job per se, but she knew she was not "a full-time person" and felt that she was not doing her best work. She also trusted that something else would come her way. In addition to her regular job, she often did weekend translations for her spiritual teacher at large conferences. She mentioned to him that she was now available to work for him if he needed her. He immediately responded that he would be happy to have her travel with him to translate throughout South and Central America. In some ways, her dream had affirmed her trust in her inner process as well as prepared her for this new relationship with her spiritual teacher.

Feminine consciousness is rooted in the heart. The feeling comes with the thought, and as the thought is spoken, the heart opens, and feeling flows to deeper, richer levels. Femininity is silenced in our culture. There is simply no time for her.
—MARION WOODMAN

As I mentioned before, masculine dream figures often serve as guides or catalysts for change. They sometimes lead the dreamer to the underworld, where she meets the Divine Feminine. I recently had a dream in which the masculine figure took me deep within a cavern to a ceremonial space where I met a Medicine Woman. There she made me aware of the necessity of doing my inner work.

I am on the back of my husband's motorcycle, holding on. We are going down a cavernous space where many people are examining ancient ceiling paintings. We travel deeper and he brings me into a ceremonial space where a Medicine Woman has prepared a pipe ceremony to give me my pipe. I am seated on the floor in front of three women. A group of people I don't see is to my left. The ceremony is very long, slow, and tedious as the Medicine Woman says the prayers. My husband stands behind me with his hand alternately on my shoulder or the small of my back the entire time. I am given medicine gifts by Joanni and Barbara, two women who have been participants in my workshops. I am particularly touched by the raven feather they give me, a symbol for me of new birth and creativity.

The medicine woman places the pipe stem in my right hand and then the ceremony stops. She says she feels that something is not in harmony with her people. She gets up and goes outside. We wait. When the Medicine Woman returns, she says she cannot continue the ceremony. I feel that something is not in harmony with me and that is why she has stopped.

At the time I had this dream, my husband of eleven years and I had just divorced. Even though we had both agreed that the marriage was over, the separation precipitated a deep descent for me. So it was no wonder that my husband in the dream was the vehicle for my journey to the underworld. He takes me to a cavern of ancient symbols (the unconscious). I meet a Medicine Woman who is an archetypal image of the divine feminine. She prepares a ceremony to give me my pipe, a symbol of the Self, the union of the masculine and feminine.

My husband stands behind me as I prepare to receive the pipe. My inner masculine backs me up to do my inner soul work. I would not have chosen to take this journey myself; I did not want to face the challenges that the process of soul growth always brings. As so often happens when we resist our growth and evolution, the outer circumstances of life demand it.

The women in the dream give me medicine gifts—I am supported by my inner feminine to do my soul work. The medicine woman gives me the pipe stem, which symbolizes the active, masculine principle. She feels, however, that I am not yet ready to receive the bowl of the pipe, which symbolizes

We return thanks to our mother, the earth, which sustains us . . .
to the wind, which, moving the air, has banished diseases . . .
to our grandfather He-no, that he has protected his grandchildren . . .
and has given to us his rain . . . to the sun, that he has looked upon the earth with a beneficent eye.
—IROQUOIS PRAYER OF THANKSGIVING

the feminine. I have more work to do to bring my unconscious into awareness before I will be ready to accept this symbol of the Self.

QUESTIONS FOR WRITING AND REFLECTION

* Identify the important men in your life. What did you learn from each one of them about the masculine?
* How do you respond when you hear the word *masculine?* What kind of feelings does the word elicit for you? What associations do you have from literature, the culture, religion, mythology, etc.?
* How would your childhood have been different or the same if you had been a boy? What freedoms, opportunities, attention, responsibility do you think you would have had?
* How would your life be different if you were a man?
* If I were a man, my priorities would be _____.
* If I were a man, I would be free to _____.
* If I were a man, I would be limited by _____.
* Identify the parts of your masculine nature that you are comfortable with. For instance, I am comfortable setting goals and following through, protecting my children, having authority, etc.
* Identify the parts of your masculine nature that you are uncomfortable with. For instance, I am uncomfortable when I feel disconnected from my feelings or I notice myself dismissing others' feelings, when I drive myself beyond my physical comfort zone, when I am perfectionistic, when my critic gets the upper hand.
* On which people in your life do you project negative masculine qualities?
* How do you cultivate the healthy aspects of your masculine nature? For instance, I have made a commitment to my creativity instead of blaming others for the time I take to meet their needs, I take care of my money issues, I am learning how to protect myself, etc.
* How do you nurture your masculine nature? For instance, you might write: I am taking a training course to develop the necessary skills to change careers after my children leave home; I am keeping track of

how I spend my time so that I can manage it better; I have installed an alarm system in my house.

GUIDED IMAGERY: INNER PROTECTOR

Close your eyes and focus your attention on your breath moving in . . . and . . . out of your nostrils. Take three deep breaths and as you exhale release any tension you may be carrying in any part of your body. As you breathe at your own rate, give yourself the suggestion that with each exhalation you move deeper and deeper into levels of consciousness where more images and memories are accessible to you.

Now imagine that you can create whatever protection you need for today. This protection will keep you safe and strong throughout all your activities and while you sleep. This Inner Protector might take the form of a person, like a strong supportive father, lover, or friend, or an imaginary animal who will accompany you and watch over you. What does your protector look like? What qualities does this protector have?

Your protector might instead take the form of an energy field that surrounds you. If so, visualize wrapping yourself with a blanket of white light. Focus your attention on your heart and see, sense, or imagine a white light that emanates from your heart area and surrounds you from your head to your feet. Continue to wrap yourself in white light until you have a cocoon of protective energy around you. When you feel protected and safe, start to count to five and slowly bring yourself back to full waking consciousness.

Write, record, or draw your experience of your Inner Protector.

After doing this exercise repeatedly, Susan, an artist in her late thirties, described having an image of covering her body with a strong paper bag made of tree bark. That day she went into the college where she taught art and was surprised to find that her department chair had given one of her classes to another faculty member without informing her. In the past she would have acquiesced to the department chair's decision, but this day, feeling calm and protected, she decided instead to quit her job. I'm not suggesting that your Inner Protector will cause you to abandon your job, but it might help you refuse to accept treatment that is destructive to your self-esteem.

ART ACTIVITY: PROTECTOR SHIELD

Create a collage of images that are symbolic of protection for you and give you strength for your journey. For example, in my shield I have images of several of my animal allies: raven, eagle, owl, dolphin, as well as the Black Madonna of LePuy, to which I made a pilgrimage. The four corners represent the four elements: water, earth, air, fire. Central to my collage is a milagro heart aflame given to me by my friend Betty. I have surrounded the heart with images of the protectors in my life, including four women in a hot tub, who I have recently called upon to keep me safe and help heal my heart.

Some women like to collage photos of all of the men and women who have been protective of them in their life or to create a fantasy protector with all the qualities you might need to help you feel safe. Another idea would be to place pictures or symbols of the men who have not been protective in your life at the bottom of your shield and do some inner work to hold them accountable. When you feel complete, and only when, forgive them and let them go.

ART ACTIVITY: COLLAGE OF THE IMPORTANT MEN IN YOUR LIFE

Create a collage of the important men in your life, thinking about what you admire about them and how they inspire you. These men may be relatives, men from history, art, literature, mythology, politics, film, and the like. Use magazine pictures, current photographs, old photographs that have been photocopied and hand-colored. Make a paper quilt or collage. Dialogue with each man as you add him to your collage. How do the men in the collage reflect aspects of yourself that you value and wish to integrate more?

TABLE OF FEMININE AND MASCULINE TRAITS

Bringing ourselves into balance involves integrating the positive aspects of what have stereotypically been described as feminine and masculine feelings and behaviors. The terms *feminine* and *masculine* are used to describe ways of being, inherent principles of human existence embodied by both women and men. They do not refer to gender. Until very recently, *feminine* has been distorted by Western culture to convey woman/weakness, while *masculine* has been distorted to convey man/strength. These words should instead refer to a continuum of attributes inherent in all human beings unlimited by gender.

Masculine consciousness often tries to help the feminine to speak. It jumps in and takes over. It does not wait for the body to know its truth. Nor does it wait for the right moment. Feminine consciousness senses timing.
—MARION WOODMAN

The following is a list of attributes that includes culturally recognizable concepts of feminine and masculine embodied by both women and men. This list is presented as an example of masculine and feminine feelings and behaviors; it is not presented to stereotype or limit the understanding of feminine and masculine. When these attributes are in balance, they contribute to the healthy functioning of the psyche. When they are out of balance, the psyche is stressed. You will notice, for example, that the attribute of being assertive and direct can become manipulative and indirect when out of balance. Complete the list of qualities that are out of balance.

FEMININE QUALITIES IN BALANCE	WHEN OUT OF BALANCE BECOME
assertive, direct	manipulative, indirect
relational	controlling
warm, nurturing	smothering
diffuse	unfocused
allowing, lets things happen	passive
acquiescent, accommodating	victim, martyr
affiliative, need to connect	dependent
bringing together, networking	
creative	
supportive	
committed, responsible	
courageous, protective	
intimate	
open, inclusive	
enfolding	
fertile	
empowered	

FEMININE QUALITIES IN BALANCE

sensual, erotic

soulful

calm, serene

empathic, compassionate

emotionally expressive

flowing, creatively changing

body-oriented

operating in cyclic time

independent, responsible for self-esteem

accepting, receptive

vulnerable

inner-focused

nonviolent

in touch with emotions, dreams, intuition

interdependent

MASCULINE QUALITIES IN BALANCE	WHEN OUT OF BALANCE BECOME
competitive	violent, domineering
decisive, intellectual	coldly rational
makes things happen	authoritarian, controlling
disciplined	rigidly adheres to law and order
protective	manipulative
compassionate, empathic	sentimental
outer-directed in general	emotionally unavailable
courageous, powerful	
supportive, instructive	
steady, ambitious	
committed, responsible	
endurance, perseverance	
entertains many points of view	
discriminates, makes distinctions	
sets limits	
rationally concerned with fairness, truth	
operating in linear time	

MASCULINE QUALITIES IN BALANCE
objective
entitled
need for autonomy, freedom, separation
independent
nurturing
sexual
strategic, goal oriented
desire to create structure

* How do you identify the feminine and masculine qualities within yourself? Make your own list.
* How do these qualities work for you and how do they hold you back?
* In which situations do you act more from your feminine nature, and in which situations do you act more from your masculine nature?
* When do you feel out of balance? When do you feel in balance?
* What can you do to bring more balance into your life?

DREAM GROUPS

Dreams are often weeks, months, or years ahead of your conscious understanding, so if you review your dreams now and then, you can sometimes perceive sequences and themes. It's surprising how an early dream suddenly can become more understandable.
—KAREN A. SIGNELL, *Wisdom of the Heart*

Dreams often give us guidance about what is happening in our psyche. As I have mentioned before, it is helpful to review your dreams at least once a year to see the themes and patterns that are emerging and any corresponding changes or stalemates that have occurred in your waking life. Many people find that telling their dreams to another person helps them clarify the dream even if the other person does not give them feedback.[1] If you are interested in feedback and are not in therapy, you may wish to start or join a dream group.

I am part of a weekly women's dream group in which each of the five members tells her dream in the present tense as if the dream is being dreamed in the present. The members who have had a strong connection to the dream respond as if it were their dream. For example, a woman might respond by saying, "If this were my dream, it would mean . . ." or "If I were in your life situation and this were my dream, it would tell me . . ." In this way, you receive another person's associations to your dream without actually having the dream analyzed or interpreted. These associations can be very helpful in giving you perspective about your own associations and interpretation. It is important to listen carefully to the essential voice of the dream even though it may be disruptive or unwanted in the dreamer's outer life.

RECORD THE DREAMS YOU HAVE WHILE WORKING WITH THIS CHAPTER.

The Sacred Marriage

7

If you care about men and women, become aware of the Tao. When
you stop trying and loosen your grip on others, life takes care of itself.
—PAMELA METZ AND JACQUELINE TOBIN, *The Tao of Women*

In myths of old, the sacred marriage of the Goddess and her son or consort represented the cyclic regeneration of life, focusing on sex, love, and regeneration. The greatest power was to give and nurture life, and the Goddess was seen as the one who gave life and took it back again so that it might be reborn. The sacred marriage was perceived as the catalyst activating new life every spring.

As society became more male centered, the sacred marriage and its focus on life—the cyclic unity of birth, sex, death, and regeneration—receded into insignificance. Memories of the sacred marriage of the Goddess and of myths and rites of sex and birth still remained, but with time the myths of a sacred union focused not between woman and man, but between man and God, a sacred marriage in which the feminine disappeared.[1] In medieval Christianity the sacred marriage underwent another radical transformation—instead of a celebration of life and love, it became a celebration of pain and death.[2]

In the world of the psyche, the sacred marriage is the marriage of ego and self. The heroine comes to understand the dynamics of her feminine and masculine natures and works to integrate them. As I wrote in the last chapter, integration requires the withdrawal of a woman's projections onto the men in her life. A women not only projects her wounded masculine nature onto men but frequently projects her unlived potential onto a man as well, hoping he will actualize her destiny. When a woman, instead, is involved in her own creative work and getting it out into the world, and has reclaimed her own feminine consciousness, both aspects of her nature become a conscious part of her personality.

Through the sacred marriage, the unity of all opposites, woman remembers her true nature. "It is a moment of recognition, a kind of remembering of that which somewhere at bottom we have always known. The current problems are not solved, the conflicts remain, but such a person's suffering, as long as [s]he does not evade it, will no longer lead to neuroses but to new life. The individual intuitively glimpses who [s]he is."[3] The Jungian analyst June Singer writes:

> A wise person once said that the goal of the masculine principle is perfection and the goal of the feminine principle is completion. If you are perfect, you cannot be complete, because you must leave out all the imperfections of your nature. If you are complete, you cannot be perfect, for being complete means that you contain good and evil, right and wrong, hope and despair. So perhaps it is best to be content with something less than perfection and something less than completion. Perhaps we need to be more willing to accept life as it comes.[4]

The sacred marriage is complete when a woman joins the two aspects of her nature; the feminine and masculine have begun to cherish each other. This is the task of the contemporary heroine. The heroine becomes the Mistress of Both Worlds; she can navigate the waters of daily life and listen to the teachings of the depths. She is the Mistress of Heaven and Earth and of the Underworld. She has gained wisdom from her experiences; she no longer needs to blame the other; she *is* the other. She brings that wisdom back to share with the world. And the women, men, and children of the world are transformed by her journey.

The result of the union of the feminine and masculine is the birth of a new entity, the divine child, the Self. The heroine is centered in the heroine's wholeness. Living responsibly from this place of consciousness, she can do something for humankind. The more conscious she is, the more possible it is to show compassion and true love for others. This is the gift that the heroine brings back to the

For men, the dark eternal woman in her many guises is the bridge to the Self. For women, she is the feminine part of the Self. In both genders, she is the creative matrix that gives birth to the new order.
—MARION WOODMAN

community from her journey. But not until she has learned to maintain her own sovereignty.

GAWAIN AND LADY RAGNELL

One of the great tales about the sacred marriage is the English tale "Gawain and Lady Ragnell," which portrays the healing of both the wounded masculine and the distorted feminine. It takes place in fourteenth-century England.[5]

One day in late summer, Gawain, the nephew of King Arthur, was with his uncle and the knights of the court at Carlisle. The king returned from the day's hunting in Inglewood looking so pale and shaken that Gawain followed him to his chamber and asked him what was the matter.

The heroic journey for women is taking the risk to love, day after day.
—KAREN SIGNELL

While out hunting alone, Arthur had been accosted by a fearsome knight of the northern lands named Sir Gromer, who sought revenge for the loss of his lands. He spared Arthur, giving him the chance to save his life by meeting him in a year at the same spot, unarmed, with the answer to the question: "What is it that women most desire, above all else?" If he found the correct answer to this question, his life would be spared.

Gawain assured Arthur that together they would be able to find the correct answer to the question, and during the next twelve months they collected answers from one corner of the kingdom to the other. As the day drew near, Arthur was worried that none of the answers had the ring of truth.

A few days before he was to meet Sir Gromer, Arthur rode out alone through the golden gorse and purple heather to a grove of great oaks. There before him stood a huge, grotesque woman. "She was almost as wide as she was high, her skin was mottled green and spikes of weedlike hair covered her head. Her face seemed more animal than human."[6] Her name was Lady Ragnell.

The woman told Arthur that she knew he was about to meet her stepbrother, Sir Gromer, and that he did not have the right answer to the question. She told him that she knew the correct answer and would tell him, if the knight Gawain would become her husband. Arthur was shocked and cried out that it was impossible; he could not give her his nephew.

She made it very clear to Arthur that she had not asked him to *give* her the knight Gawain. "If Gawain himself agrees to marry me, I will give you the answer. Those are my terms."[7] She told him that she would meet him at the same spot the next day, and she disappeared into the oak grove.

Arthur was crestfallen because he could not consider asking his nephew to give his own life in marriage to this ugly woman in order to save himself. Gawain rode out from the castle to meet the king, and when he saw him looking pale and strained, he asked Arthur what had happened. At first Arthur declined to tell him, but when he finally told Gawain the terms of Lady Ragnell's proposal, Gawain was delighted that he would be able to save Arthur's life. When Arthur pleaded with him not to sacrifice himself, Gawain answered that it was his choice and his decision. He would return with Arthur the next day to Lady Ragnell and agree to marry her on condition that the answer she gave saved Arthur's life.

Arthur and Gawain met Lady Ragnell and agreed to her conditions. The following day Arthur rode alone, unarmed, to Inglewood to meet Sir Gromer. Arthur first tried all of his other answers, and just as Sir Gromer lifted his sword to cleave Arthur in two, Arthur added, "I have one more answer. What a woman desires above all else is the power of sovereignty—the right to exercise her own will."[8] Sir Gromer, angered because he knew that Arthur must have learned the true answer from Lady Ragnell, swore an oath against his stepsister and ran off into the forest.

Gawain held to his promise and married Lady Ragnell that day. After the wedding feast, which was attended in shock and uneasy silence by the knights and ladies of Arthur's court, the married couple retired to their chamber. Lady Ragnell asked Gawain to kiss her. Gawain went to her immediately and kissed her. When he stepped back, there was a slender young woman with gray eyes smiling back at him.

Gawain was shocked, and wary of her sorcery, and asked what had happened to effect such a dramatic change. She told him that her stepbrother had always hated her and had told his mother, who had a knowledge of sorcery, to change her into a monstrous creature who could only be released if the greatest knight in Britain willingly chose her for his bride. Gawain asked her why Sir Gromer hated her so.

"He thought me bold and unwomanly because I defied him. I refused his commands both for my property and my person."[9] Gawain smiled at her in admiration and marveled that the spell was now broken. "Only in part," she replied. "You have a choice, dear Gawain, which way I will be. Would you have me in this, my own shape, at night and my former ugly shape by day? Or would you have me grotesque at night in our chamber, and my own shape in the castle by day? Think carefully before you choose."[10]

Gawain thought for a moment, then knelt before her, touched her hand, and told her it was a choice that he could not make because it was her choice only to make. He told her that whatever she chose he would willingly support. Ragnell radiated her joy. "You have answered well, dearest Gawain, for your answer has broken Gromer's evil spell completely. The last condition he set has been met! For he said that if, after marriage to the greatest knight in Britain, my husband freely gave me the power of choice, the power to exercise my own free will, the wicked enchantment would be broken forever."[11]

Lady Ragnell and Gawain were united in a sacred marriage of two equals who had made a free and conscious choice to come together. Lady Ragnell had been bewitched by her stepbrother for asserting her will and protecting her sexuality. Gawain did not impose his will on her but gave her the freedom to transform her disfiguration. Ragnell had the ability to save the king, and Gawain had the wisdom to recognize the sovereignty of the feminine. Together they found healing love. In some versions of the legend, Lady Ragnell is the Grail Goddess who carries the Grail into the castle of the Fisher King, and Gawain is both her healer and her lover.

Like Lady Ragnell, to live heroically a woman must belong to herself alone; she must have sovereignty over her own life. She must utilize the sword of discernment to cut away the ego bonds that hold her to the past and find out what serves her soul's purpose. She must release resentment toward the mother, put aside blame and idealization of the father, and find the courage to face her own darkness. She must be determined, brave, and willing to overcome her fears to forge new inner pathways.

> Each of us, as we journey through life, has the opportunity to find and to give his or her unique gift. Whether that gift is great or small in the eyes of the world does not matter at all—not at all. It is through the finding and the giving that we may come to know the joy that lies at the center of both the dark times and the light.
>
> —HELEN LUKE,
>   *An African Tale*

The task of today's heroine is to mine the silver and gold within herself. As she honors her body and soul as well as her mind, she heals the split within herself and the culture. Women today are acquiring the courage to express their vision, the strength to set limits, and the willingness to take responsibility for themselves and others in a new way. They are reminding people of their origins, the necessity to live mindfully, and their obligation to preserve life on earth.

RITUAL: CIRCLE OF STONES

At a certain point in your life it is time to let the people you have held accountable for wounding or disappointing you off the hook. These are the "ego bonds" that hold you to the past. Something may have happened to you in a relationship with a particular person that has altered your life in a deep, meaningful way. Perhaps you carry the wounds of sexual or physical abuse, abandonment, betrayal, divorce, or a loved one's death. The Circle of Stones is a ritual you can do to make peace with past relationships. Without such a process you may remain stuck as a victim, clinging to suffering or fantasy.

In the circle of stones ritual you will have an opportunity to create a container in which to engage in a dialogue with the person or people with whom you have unfinished business without actually having them present. After you have said all that you need to say and have heard all that you need to hear, you can let them go. As you release each person you hold accountable for your pain (or in the case of a loved one who has died, for aspects of your life you do not feel that you can manage on your own), you are free to move forward on your journey.

Find a private place in nature where you can sit uninterrupted. It is important that you find a safe place to do your work. You will be creating a sacred, ritual space. Spend time gathering stones that represent each person with whom you would like to dialogue. Let the stones present themselves to you without your doing the choosing. The shape, color, or size of a particular stone will remind you of each person.

When you have collected your stones, find one more that represents yourself. Return to the place where you are about to create your circle of stones and smudge the area with sage for purification. Then assemble the stones in such a way that you are part of the circle. For example, you might have a stone for your mother, father, spouse, child, and friend, as well as one for yourself. Sit in the circle with all six stones. Five or six stones is a manageable number, but you may find that you wish instead to focus on only one or two relationships. (You can always increase the number of stones.)

Take a moment to close your eyes, center yourself, and pray for guidance. Then choose a stone with which to begin your dialogue. Tell this relative or friend of the wounds you have experienced in your relationship, how you have felt disappointed, abused, dismissed, possessed, or otherwise harmed by him or her. Talk about your yearnings for connection and how you have been thwarted. Acknowledge what you have appreciated. Now, listen to what your relative or friend has to say to you. Allow a dialogue to evolve so that you can say everything you have always wanted to say as well as hear his or her response.

Continue with this dialogue until you have nothing more to say to this person. When you feel complete, you may wish to express your gratitude for his or her presence, and tell the person that you release him or her from the wounds and disappointments you have attributed to your relationship. From this point forward, you no longer hold the person accountable for your life. You are responsible for your own destiny.

In this same way, address each of the stones in your circle. Talk, cry, yell. Make sure you give yourself permission to speak your truth and to hear theirs. You don't have to be reasonable. Leave the stone that represents yourself until last. When you are ready to dialogue with your stone, tell yourself of your shame, anger, longings, lusts, disappointments. You may find that dialoguing with yourself in this way presents the greatest challenge. Forgive yourself for the ways in which you have let yourself down. Then acknowledge yourself for your growth, accomplishments, creativity, and wisdom as well as for your desire to heal yourself. When you are complete with each person in the circle, including yourself, bless them all in your own way, and open the circle. Return the stones back to nature. You are then free to go.

ART ACTIVITY: MASKS

In our culture many of us wear masks to conceal who we are from ourselves as well as from others. The maskmaker Valerie T. Bechtol created the following

A workshop participant with her completed mask.

exercise for participants in our workshops to focus on the two aspects of themselves, inner and outer. In creating your own mask, think about who you present to the outside world, your outer mask, and who you are deep within yourself, your inner mask. Although it is possible to make the mask by yourself, I suggest that you make the mask with a partner. You may wish to review the Descent and the images that emerged during the guided imagery of the Descent to remind yourself of the many masks you show to the world.

For each mask you will need two rolls of three-inch-wide gauze impregnated with plaster and cut to different lengths (Johnson and Johnson is a good brand and is available at some pharmacies and art stores), scissors, petroleum jelly, and baby oil, a bathing cap, and a bucket of warm water.

Cut larger pieces of the gauze for the forehead and chin, three-inch squares for the cheeks, nose, and eyes, and narrow strips for the bridge of the nose and lips. Cut enough gauze pieces for three layers.

Make the mask outside or put plastic down on the floor of your work area. Push your hair (or your partner's hair) into the bathing cap and use petroleum jelly around the edge of your hairline; cover your face with baby oil. Dip a large strip of plaster gauze into warm water and apply it to your forehead. Use your fingers to smooth out any bumps in the plaster. Begin at your forehead and work your way down your face to your chin with each successive plaster strip. Always overlap each strip. Once you have completed the first layer from the forehead to the chin, repeat the same for the next two layers. Cover your eyes if you are comfortable doing so and leave breathing holes in the nostrils of your mask. The first layer of plaster strips creates the casting of your face, and the next two layers reinforce the mask.

Allow the mask to "set" (approximately five minutes) before you remove it from your own or your partner's face. The easiest way to remove it is to create space under the entire edge of the mask with your finger and then gently pull the mask off. While it is still wet you can finish the edges of the entire mask by folding narrow strips of the plaster gauze along the edges to reinforce any weak spots.

Put the mask outside in the sun to dry; in wet climates put the mask on a cookie sheet in a warm oven at 200 degrees for twenty to thirty minutes. After the mask dries, coat it with a polymer medium such as Rhoplex to seal it. The plaster dries from the inside out, so be sure that it is dry.

After you have made your mask and sealed it, spend time with it before you paint it. Everyone is always surprised at what the inside of the mask looks like. Play with your mask, sleep with it, dream with it. Place the mask close to where you sleep and take a few moments before you go to bed to hold it and look at it inside and out.

In the morning, meditate while holding the mask. Pay attention to any feelings, memories, images that emerge during your meditation. If you have a deep relationship with nature or animals, you may wish your mask to reflect this connection. Make notes about what is important to you to incorporate in your mask.

You will need materials such as acrylic paints, brushes, Elmer's glue or a glue gun, personal symbols, fur, feathers, hair, veiling, mirrors, buttons, and glitter. Paint the interior of your mask first—the inner you, not the mask you show to the outer world: your deepest feelings, secrets, dreams, the part of you that only you know. Don't judge. After the inner mask has dried, paint the outer mask, the face you wish to show to the outer world. Another suggestion is to paint your mask as aspects of your feminine and masculine natures (female on the outside, male on the inside, or vice versa).

When the mask is painted, you may wish to cut open the space for your eyes, if you have not already created eye holes. Decorate the mask by gluing on personal symbols such as hair, yarn, or veiling. Attach elastic near the cheekbones for wearing the mask or a stick at the chin for a handheld mask.

You may also choose to create a casting of a part of your body other than your face. In one weekend workshop, a young woman who was nine months pregnant made a casting of her swollen belly; in another, a middle-aged woman who had just adopted a child made a casting of her breasts and belly. Have fun!

RITUAL: THE SACRED MARRIAGE

The hierosgamos or sacred marriage has its roots far back in primitive belief systems, where our ancestors were convinced that the union of the human woman and man reflected and maintained the coming together of earth and heaven.

When we are in love and totally absorbed in being with that person, doing something that nourishes the soul, we are out of ordinary time and in the Motherworld.
—JEAN SHINODA BOLEN

The marriage and its consummation were seen as absolutely necessary to ensure the continued union of Mother Earth and Father Sky and the resulting fertility of the land. To ensure your continued growth and creativity and to honor your journey, create a ritual that joins together the two great energies within you, your masculine and feminine essences.

Elements similar to those suggested below were used in rituals from primitive times to the present to acknowledge the sacred marriage. You may wish to incorporate them into your ritual of commitment to yourself.

* Gather plants or flowers, candles, clothing, jewelry, favorite foods, and music that you wish to use in your ritual.
* Beautify and prepare your space: cleanse the area first by burning sage, and assemble the art, photographs, colors, and symbols that are important to you. If you have an altar, clean it and put fresh flowers on it.
* Call upon the spirit of the goddess Aphrodite or the spirit of Divine Love to bless you in your sacred marriage with yourself.

In primitive marriages, one of the first ritual elements was for both members of the prospective couple to renounce their previous state of being. This symbolic rite of separation was the first act of removing oneself from one's initial family. For either the woman or the man, this often meant ripping up items of clothing or giving away clothes; cutting, breaking, or giving away a special childhood treasure; cutting the hair; removing jewelry; consecrating something of their previous life to a deity; changing food habits; washing or being washed; passing through a threshold (doorway, gate, or steps); or breaking a thread.

Throughout the stages of your journey, you have already performed rituals of separation in completing the severance ritual and the circle of stones ritual; in so doing you have renounced a former state of being. As a further statement about breaking your ties to the past, incorporate one of the following into your ritual:

* Pass through or cross a threshold.
* Break or give away a childhood treasure.
* Cut your hair.
* Rip up a piece of clothing or a photograph that represents your former self.

Before a marriage rite occurs, it is presumed that the couple has already fallen in love. In the case of the inner marriage, it is important that you consciously accept yourself as you are, just as you would accept and love a close friend. You are comfortable spending time with yourself; you have compassion for your imperfections. You appreciate your humor, passion, and uniqueness. You experience yourself as your own best friend. To express this stage, you might do one or more of the following:

* Light a fire in your hearth and sprinkle ashes from the fire in your garden.
* Write a love letter to yourself expressing appreciation for who you are.
* Draw a bath with your favorite bath salts (salt symbolizes Eros and wisdom).
* Light candles around the tub and play relaxing music while you bathe.
* Dry yourself out in the sun.

The rite of marriage in primitive times often included one of the following: eating a meal together; exchanging bracelets, rings, or clothing; binding oneself to one's loved one with a knot or cord; being wrapped together in a single piece of cloth or clothing; drinking wine (or other libation) from the same container; and saying vows in front of family and friends. For this part of your inner ritual:

* Prepare a special feast to celebrate your union with yourself.
* Put on a new dress or other article of clothing that you have made, received, or purchased for your wedding ceremony.
* Prepare a favorite drink and pour it into a goblet that you have acquired for your ceremony.
* Create or purchase a ring or bracelet that represents your marriage with yourself.
* Write vows or promises to yourself, the Beloved. Your vows incorporate commitments to the parts of yourself that you wish to acknowledge and strengthen. Here is an example:

My Beloved,

I promise to accept your feelings no matter how uncomfortable they might be.

I promise to be attentive to and respond to your needs.

I promise to love you for who you are, not what you do.

I promise to keep you safe from people and situations that endanger your well-being.

I promise to send your critic on vacation whenever she interferes with your creative process.

I promise to celebrate your creativity and to nurture your continued growth.

I promise to honor your body and let you rest when you are tired.

I promise to exercise, eat nourishing foods, and attend to your health.

I promise to schedule unscheduled time for you to hang out and "smell the roses."

I promise to nurture your spiritual life.

I promise to laugh and have fun.

I promise to take you seriously [or less seriously, depending upon what you need].

I promise to review and renew my vows each time I forget to keep them.

One woman wrote her vows with succinct eloquence: "I vow to love my inner self above all others, to cherish myself, to honor and obey the choices of my heart."

You may wish to invite close friends, family members, or a circle of women to witness your ritual, or you may prefer to celebrate your sacred marriage in a favorite location by yourself. If you invite others, gift them with something from your past, or ask them to bring some symbol or gift to honor your journey and the changes you have made. Some women have created rituals in which they ask a close friend to stand in for the masculine part of themselves while they exchange vows. They then feast, dance, and celebrate together.

You will find that dreams truly inform you in little ways, and sometimes they gradually lead you to follow the deeper currents of your life. This happens when certain dreams grip your attention. You no longer just look at them with detachment as if they were interesting movies, but you are moved by them.
—KAREN SIGNELL

The final rite of marriage in primitive times was that of sexual union. In the inner marriage this can be expressed on a literal level through making love with yourself or more symbolically through a ritual that incorporates one of the following:

* Change the direction of your bed.
* Buy new bedding, a comforter, or a quilt.
* Buy yourself a special nightgown or silk pajamas.
* Wear earrings or other jewelry that represent the merging of the moon and the sun (feminine and masculine).[12]
* Review your most treasured wish or blessing for yourself and choose one that you want to actualize. On the full moon, go outside with a glass of water, speak your wish or blessing into the water, and leave it under the moonlight. In the morning when you first wake up, drink the moonlit water, which has assimilated your wish.
* Write your intentions on strips of cloth and hang them on the branches of your favorite tree.

Before you fall asleep on your wedding night, request a dream that celebrates your inner marriage.

DREAMS

Dreams record the process of individuation and the movement of the ego toward consciousness of the inner self. In dreamwork, as in maskmaking, we learn to look at the hidden parts of ourselves—feelings, opinions, ideals, personalities— that we may be unconscious of during our waking life. Because our conscious minds can focus on only a limited aspect of our total being at any given time, we look to our dreams for a record of our journey to make these hidden aspects of our self conscious.

RECORD THE DREAMS YOU HAVE WHILE WORKING WITH THIS CHAPTER.

Conclusion

So the heroine? Who needs a counterpart to the hero? I see a vastly different woman coming to be out of the rubble that most of the heroes have left after them. One who will not be "going" anywhere (she can spiral to her heart's content dancing the days away) but who will have caught on little by little, in company with other women, that there is no place to go to, and no one to be. Maybe that's the essence of the way that lies ahead for woman . . . to know that she "is." That ought to be enough to keep her busy for at least a couple of centuries!
—FIONA O'CONNELL

When you return from the Heroine's Journey, you discover not so much that you have found the answers as that you have become more comfortable living the questions. As you look at your life through the lens of the Heroine's Journey, you probably have greater appreciation for the various twists and turns in the fabric of your personal story. In addition, the questions posed in chapter 1—Why are you here? How have you made your way through life? What tribe do you belong to? Where and how do you fit within the greater scheme of things?—may now have more meaning for you. I hope that these final exercises give you the freedom to rest in the assurance that you need not journey anywhere outside yourself to be you.

QUESTIONS FOR WRITING AND REFLECTION

Reflect on the following questions in preparation for writing or recording your personal myth.

* What core beliefs dominated your family dynamics? For instance, "We're one, big, happy family," "Never tell a secret to anyone outside the family," "Our family doesn't engage in conflict," "They're out to get us," "The women in our family are doormats," "My sister/brother is the smart/pretty/creative one," "The men in our family are all successful," "No one in our family can carry a tune."
* What part of the myth did you carry as a child in the family, and what part do you carry now?
* What part of your family myth have you rejected?
* What positive messages did you get from your family?
* "What bargain did you make in the family? Family bargains are implicit agreements that you, the child, will be rewarded for certain behaviors. For instance, "If I don't complain about Mommy's anger, I'll get Daddy's attention," "If I take Mommy's side, she will cuddle with me," "If I buy Mommy candy, she won't yell at me," "If I'm quiet and always do what Daddy wants, he will love me."
* How do you still enact these family bargains in your adult relationships?
* Did you experience a "fall from grace," a time when you lost your innocence in your family's eyes?
* Do you remember a time when you became aware of "faults" in yourself, ways of behaving that you were not proud of (lying, cheating, mistreating or betraying a friend)? How did you feel about these self-discoveries? Did you develop a pattern of blaming others, blaming yourself, or making constructive changes in your life?
* When did you discover the limitations in your mother, father, best friend, God, a hero/heroine? How were you

The stories people tell have a way of taking care of them. If stories come to you, care for them. And learn to give them away where they are needed. Sometimes a person needs a story more than food to stay alive.

—CROW AND WEASEL

affected by your discovery? Did you draw some unconscious conclusion such as "I cannot trust the person I love most," "It's dangerous to need someone," "I can't depend on anyone else but myself"?

* How did those limitations wound you? What are the patterns of your life that were started by this wounding?
* What are the disappointments of your mother/father that you still carry? In what ways are you still living their unlived story?
* Did you have any "peak experiences" growing up that awakened you to a sense of your life's purpose? To what degree have you been able to respond to this "call"?
* Did you take the Heroine's Journey consciously, or were you propelled into it? What insights do you now have about yourself as a result of taking this inner journey?
* What fears have you overcome?
* What strengths have you developed?
* What sacrifices have you made? What have been the rewards?
* Is there a symbol or image that has sustained you thus far on your journey?
* Where are you in the process of healing the mother-daughter split? (For most women, this is an ongoing process that takes time and patience.)
* What difficulties have you encountered as you integrate the learnings of your journey into your everyday life?
* What is the new myth you are creating for yourself?

> *In the deepest sense, leaving one's parents means to surpass, perhaps by transforming, the central striving at the core of the parents' lives. One looks for themes and patterns underlying surface attitudes and actions, which means that one must know oneself and one's parents very well.*
> —LINDA SUSSMAN

WRITING EXERCISE: YOUR PERSONAL MYTH

Write your personal myth as a short story, fairy tale, or poem.

A personal myth is the story you tell yourself and others that contains answers about the meaning of your life. It reflects the beliefs, feelings, and images you hold about yourself and is significantly influenced by your family, friends, and culture. As you review your answers to the questions in the previous section, you will begin to discover the myth that is central to your life.

The following is an example of how a former writing student and author, Samantha Dunn, approached her personal myth.

THE FAIRY WHO FELL TO EARTH

Long ago in a land of verdant oak hills and fresh stream waters, there lived a *bean sidhe,* a woman of the fairy. This fairy's eyes were jade stone, her hair was a henna curtain collected with a silver clasp at the nape of her neck, and her skin was fresh cream collected from fat cows.

She could watch the town's women as a leaf on a tree, as a mouse in the comer, as a rabbit in the garden, and she saw that she was more beautiful than they. Still, these mortals had men to love them, homes to keep, and children to feed from their breast. And although the fairy was the perfection of beauty itself, and had special fairy powers and wisdom earned from centuries, she too wanted to be a human woman.

> *A story is a medicine that greases and hoists the pulleys, shows us the way out, down, in and around, cuts for us fine wide doors in previously blank walls, doors which, lead us to our own knowing.*
> —CLARISSA PINKOLA ESTES

When she told the queen fairy of her desire, the queen told her: "Go then and live as an equal among the humans. But be warned that your resplendence will be smashed if a human man rejects you. If so, you will wander the earth as a crone for seven millennia until you find redemption in the love of another."

The fairy was far too proud—as all fairies are—to believe that anyone could reject her. "If there will be rejection it will be me to decide whom I want and whom I don't," said she. And with careless arrogance she became human.

Then she lived as any woman: she boiled her cabbage, tended her garden, fed stray dogs, and scattered oatmeal for the birds. But it wasn't until she saw the plowman's son, Sean O'Leary, that she felt the spark of danger and ecstasy of longing that is the greatest thrill of being human.

Sean O'Leary had hair a luscious tangle of onyx and his frame was as muscular and mighty as any thoroughbred's. His eyes of lapis blue soon turned of their own accord to the fairy and he fell in love.

"Let me kiss you, my black Irish rose," he told her, making no mention of bands of gold or promises of forever.

The fairy, whose human womanness was new and artificial, did not know about these bands and did not demand promises. So she gave herself freely to the handsome O'Leary, expecting only fairness and equality.

Within weeks the moon had passed, and she sensed a sprout of life within her, so she told O'Leary of the artwork their love had created. "Get from me, you slut," said he. "I do not know you, I do not own you, you do not exist." And then he laughed and walked away.

Suffocation, loss of reason, or an eternal curse on the bloodline was the penalty for any human who injured the pride of a fairy, with or without malice aforethought. But this fairy had relinquished her abilities in order to know humanness, and could do nothing but feel the knife twist of pain in her heart.

The old queen fairy's admonishment was realized, for soon the fairy felt wrinkles crack her face, her spine became gnarled and tortured, and she saw her red hair fall out, replaced with soiled straw. The flowers wilted on the plants in her garden, birds fled from her withered hands, and dogs yelped at her ugliness.

She descended to the cellar of her cottage and hoped to know mortality. But the gleam of life that had begun to grow within her stayed and sustained her even though she did not want it to.

She was alone, filthy, and delirious with agony when the life force decided to make its entrance into the world. She managed to collect it in rags and look into its red and wizened face.

"I tried to kill myself and you, so be it if you hate me," she lamented. "Forever there will be nothing for me anyway."

But the small life lifted its fist to her and, despite her ugly countenance, clung to her for love. The child gave her her love without question, for this fairy had created her.

Seas of tears sprang from the fairy's eyes, but rather than falling on the parched and drought-seized cheeks of a crone, they cascaded down a polished face, fell upon rosebud lips. She looked at her hands, strong and sculptured, and knew she was once again a fairy.

"I am again my true nature," she laughed, and said to her daughter, "Now I can give you everything."

And from that day forward, she wanted only to be her fairy self.

GUIDED IMAGERY: MANDALA

The more we can live in partnership with our unconscious, the less discord we will have within ourselves.[1] The more we consult it and cooperate with it, the more we will be able to realize the full potential that is us. As we integrate material from the unconscious into our conscious mind, we finally become aware of the wholeness of our total being in unity with the cosmos. This is called the Self. The Self is represented by the circle, a mandala (a circle divided into four parts), the square, and the union of the royal couple.[2]

The Self is whatever we experience that is greater than our small selves through which we know that there is something meaningful to our existence.
—JEAN SHINODA BOLEN

Sit in a comfortable position and close your eyes. Begin to breathe in and out through your nostrils, giving yourself the suggestion that with each exhalation you become more and more relaxed. With each exhalation you move into deeper and deeper levels of consciousness where more images and memories are accessible to you. Now take a deep breath . . . hold it . . . and relax your breath with a slight sigh. Good. Let's do that again. Take a deep breath . . . hold it . . . relax. Good. Again, take a deep breath . . . hold it . . . and relax. Good.

Now breathe at your own rate and focus your attention at the heart center in the middle of your chest. Imagine a circle in the middle of your heart that slowly begins to expand with each breath that you take. As you breathe, the circle begins to grow, getting larger and larger, until the circle surrounds your entire body. (Pause.)

As you continue to breathe, your circle continues to expand until it encompasses all of your family and friends, animals, plants, trees, rocks, the earth and sea, the sky, sun, moon, and stars and finally incorporates the entire universe. (Pause.) With each breath you take, you and the universe become one, in energy, spirit, and love. (Pause.) Continue to breathe into your circle as you imagine yourself as Mandala, being both the center and the whole of the universe. (Pause.) Now begin to bring your awareness back to your heart center, still feeling your connection with all sentient life.

When you are ready, slowly start to bring yourself back to full waking consciousness. As you count to five, become aware of your physical body and your breath. (Pause.) Open your eyes at five, feeling relaxed and alert.

Choose a piece of white or black paper to draw or cut out a circle. Use oil pastels, markers, or paints to illustrate your mandala.

Like a mandala, the following dream illustrates the integration of the parts of the self. You will notice that one aspect of the dreamer hears the music of the spheres in her head; the other aspect translates it into a visual form. Together they work to create completion, wholeness, and joy for all those who listen. The dreamer is free to be as wildly talented as she is because she can trust that within herself are the resources to actualize her potential.

> I am traveling with two people. One of them is a very gifted composer, a wild talent, a recognized genius. I watch her as she performs and I am awed at how much she is a part of the music she creates. I see how those who hear her music are moved by it. She always stays at a distance.
>
> At one of her concerts, I look to my right and see a man holding a beautiful, cylindrical object, like a drum. It is made of rich, glossy wood and has intricate designs carved into it. He is the "diagramist" and this is the device he uses to diagram the musician's compositions. He himself is very talented. He has several "fonts" and the sheets of music that emerge from his device are beautifully proportioned and visually perfect. I understand that the work of the diagramist allows the composer the freedom to be the wild, almost ethereal talent she is, because the diagramist will capture the music on paper and make of it another form of art, allowing it to endure.

DREAMS

If we look at our dreams over time, we begin to see the journey we are taking toward the evolution of the Self. Review the dreams you have recorded in this book and celebrate your journey!

Notes

INTRODUCTION

1. D. Stephenson Bond, *Living Myth: Personal Meaning as a Way of Life* (Boston: Shambhala Publications, 1993), 109.
2. See Linda Sussman, *The Speech of the Grail* (Hudson, N.Y.: Lindisfarne Press, 1995), 7–8.
3. Robert A. Johnson, *Inner Work* (San Francisco: Harper & Row, 1986), 45.
4. Ibid.

CHAPTER 1. SEPARATING FROM THE FEMININE AND IDENTIFYING WITH THE MASCULINE

1. Marion Woodman, *Leaving My Father's House* (Boston: Shambhala Publications, 1992), 13.
2. Daryl Sharp, *Jung Lexicon* (Toronto: Inner City Books, 1991), 29.
3. Carl Jung, *Freud and Psychoanalysis* (Princeton, NJ: Princeton University Press, Bollingen Series 20, 1961), 323.
4. Harriet Goldhor Lerner, *Women in Therapy* (New York: Harper & Row, 1988), 58.
5. Mary Pipher, *Reviving Ophelia* (New York: Putnam Publishing Group, 1994), 40.
6. Ibid., 39.
7. Ibid.
8. Ibid., 22.
9. Maureen Murdock, *Fathers' Daughters: Transforming the Father-Daughter Relationship* (New York: Fawcett Columbine, 1996), 11.

10. Ibid., 8.
11. Johnson, *Inner Work*, 69.

CHAPTER 2. THE ROAD OF TRIALS

1. Kathleen Noble, *The Sound of a Silver Horn* (New York: Fawcett Columbine, 1994), 67.
2. Hal Stone and Sidra Stone, *Embracing Your Inner Critic* (San Francisco: HarperCollins, 1993), 103.
3. Carol Heilbrun, *Writing a Woman's Life* (New York: Ballantine Books, 1988), 130.
4. For an in-depth analysis of Psyche and Eros, see Robert A. Johnson, *She: Understanding Feminine Psychology* (San Francisco: Harper & Row, 1977).
5. Christopher Vogler, *The Writer's Journey* (Studio City, CA: Michael Wiese Productions, 1992), 51.
6. For an in-depth analysis of Bluebeard, see Clarissa Pinkola Estes, *Women Who Run with the Wolves* (New York: Ballantine Books, 1992).
7. Johnson, *Inner Work*, 52.
8. Ibid., 56.
9. Ibid., 65.

CHAPTER 3. INITIATION AND DESCENT

1. Woodman, *Leaving My Father's House*, 115.
2. Gail Sheehy, *New Passages* (New York: Random House, 1995), 180.
3. Ann Mankowitz, *Change of Life: A Psychological Study of Dreams and Menopause* (Toronto: Inner City Books, 1984), 44.
4. Karen Kaigler-Walker, *Positive Aging: Every Woman's Quest for Wisdom and Beauty* (Berkeley: Conari Press, 1997), 2.
5. Helen Luke, *Woman, Earth, and Spirit* (New York: Crossroad, 1984), 56.
6. For an in-depth analysis of the myth of Inanna's descent, see Sylvia Brinton Perera, *Descent to the Goddess* (Toronto: Inner City Books, 1981), 13.
7. Ibid., 65.
8. Ibid., 15.
9. Murray Stein, *In Midlife* (Woodstock, CT: Spring Publications, 1983), 34.
10. Estes, *Women Who Run with the Wolves*, 67.
11. Bond, *Living Myth*, 104.
12. Perera, *Descent to the Goddess*, 55.
13. Ibid., 81.
14. Ibid., 91.
15. Fiona O'Connell, "I come from a dark house" (1997). By permission of the author.

16. Johnson, *Inner Work*, 100.
17. Ibid., 87.
18. Ibid., 94.
19. Ibid., 96.
20. Ibid.

CHAPTER 4. URGENT YEARNING TO RECONNECT WITH THE FEMININE

1. Marion Woodman, *The Pregnant Virgin* (Toronto: Inner City Books, 1985), 58.
2. Marion Woodman and Elinor Dickson, *Dancing in the Flames* (Boston: Shambhala Publications, 1996), 52.
3. Jean Shinoda Bolen, "Intersection of the Timeless with Time: Where Two Worlds Come Together," Address to Annual Association for Transpersonal Psychology Conference, Monterey, CA, August 6, 1988.
4. The Brothers Grimm, *The Complete Grimm's Fairy Tales* (New York: Pantheon Books, 1994), 160.
5. Ibid.
6. Ibid., 161.
7. Ibid.
8. Ibid.
9. Ibid.
10. Estes, *Women Who Run with the Wolves*, 393.
11. Ibid., 416.
12. Ibid., 419.
13. Ibid., 441.
14. Ibid., 449.
15. My gratitude to Valerie T. Bechtol for the exquisite work she does with spirit dolls in our workshops and for allowing me to use her notes for this exercise.
16. Karen A. Signell, *Wisdom of the Heart* (New York: Bantam Books, 1990), 36.

CHAPTER 5. HEALING THE MOTHER-DAUGHTER SPLIT

1. Estella Lauter, *Women as Mythmakers* (Bloomington: Indiana University Press, 1984), 170.
2. May Sarton, from "The Invocation to Kali," in Laura Chester and Sharon Barba, eds., *Rising Tides: Twentieth Century American Women Poets* (New York: Washington Square Press, 1973), 67.
3. The Tale of Mesmeranda is adapted from Diane Wolkstein, *The Magic Orange Tree and Other Haitian Folk Tales* (New York: Knopf, 1978).
4. Woodman, *Pregnant Virgin*, 10.

5. Woodman and Dickson, *Dancing in the Flames,* 26–27.
6. Tina Michelle Datsko, "Momma and the Death Boutique," in *Spiralling to the Light* (1997). By permission of the author.

CHAPTER 6. HEALING THE WOUNDED MASCULINE

1. Signell, *Wisdom of the Heart,* 19.

CHAPTER 7. THE SACRED MARRIAGE

1. Riane Eisler, *Sacred Pleasure* (San Francisco: HarperCollins, 1996), 142.
2. Ibid., 152.
3. Luke, *Woman, Earth, and Spirit,* 63.
4. June Singer, "A Silence of the Soul," *Quest* 2, no. 2 (summer 1989): 32.
5. Ethel Johnston Phelps, *The Maid of the North* (New York: Holt, Rinehart, and Winston, 1981).
6. Ibid., 37.
7. Ibid., 38.
8. Ibid., 40.
9. Ibid., 43.
10. Ibid., 44.
11. Ibid.
12. In preparation for the Ritual of the Sacred Marriage, I had the delightful surprise of finding a ring at a crafts fair that represents the union of the sun and the moon. The ring bears the image of Juno (Juno Lucina was the Roman goddess of celestial light) embraced by two moonstones. It was designed by Denise Leader.

CHAPTER 8. CONCLUSION

1. Johnson, *Inner Work,* 5.
2. Ibid., 49.

Selected Bibliography

Anderson, Lorraine, ed. *Sisters of the Earth*. New York: Vintage, 1991.

Arguelles, Jose, and Miriam Arguelles. *Mandala*. Berkeley: Shambhala Publications, 1972.

Bly, Carol. *The Passionate, Accurate Story*. Minneapolis: Milkweed Editions, 1990.

Boer, Charles, trans. "The Hymn to Demeter." In *Homeric Hymns*. 2nd ed. rev. Irving, Tex.: Spring Publications, 1979.

Bolen, Jean Shinoda. *Crossing to Avalon: A Woman's Midlife Pilgrimage*. San Francisco: HarperSanFrancisco, 1994.

Bond, D. Stephenson. *Living Myth: Personal Meaning as a Way of Life*. Boston: Shambhala Publications, 1993.

Cameron, Julia, with Mark Bryan. *The Artist's Way: A Spiritual Path to Higher Creativity*. New York: G. P. Putnam's Sons, 1992.

Campbell, Joseph. *The Hero with a Thousand Faces*. Bollingen Series 17. Princeton: Princeton University Press, 1949.

Chicago, Judy. *The Dinner Party*. New York: Anchor Books, 1996.

De Puy, Candace, and Dana Dovitch. *The Healing Choice*. New York: Fireside, 1997.

Duerk, Judith. *Circle of Stones: Woman's Journey to Herself*. San Diego: LuraMedia, 1989.

Eisler, Riane. *Sacred Pleasure*. San Francisco: HarperCollins, 1996.

Estes, Clarissa Pinkola. *Women Who Run with the Wolves*. New York: Ballantine Books, 1992.

———. *Women Who Run with the Wolves*. Sounds True. Audio cassette no. A069.

———. *In the House of the Riddle Mother*. Sounds True. Audio cassette no. A152.

Gimbutas, Marija. *The Goddesses and Gods of Old Europe*. Berkeley and Los Angeles: University of California Press, 1982.

————. *The Language of the Goddess.* San Francisco: Harper & Row, 1989.

Grimm, The Brothers. *The Complete Grimm's Fairy Tales.* New York: Pantheon Press, 1994.

Johnson, Robert A. *She: Understanding Feminine Psychology.* San Francisco: Harper & Row, 1977.

————. *Inner Work: Using Dreams and Active Imagination for Personal Growth.* San Francisco: Harper & Row, 1986.

Markova, Dawna. No *Enemies Within.* Berkeley: Conari Press, 1994.

Meador, Betty De Shang. *Uncursing the Dark.* Wilmette, Ill.: Chiron Publications, 1992.

Metz, Pamela K., and Jacqueline L. Tobin. *The Tao of Women.* Atlanta, Ga.: Humanics Trade, 1995.

Murdock, Maureen. *Fathers' Daughters: Transforming the Father-Daughter Relationship.* New York: Fawcett Columbine, 1996.

————. *The Heroine's Journey.* Boston: Shambala Publications, 1990.

————. *Spinning Inward: Using Guided Imagery with Children.* Boston: Shambhala Publications, 1987.

Noble, Kathleen. *The Sound of a Silver Horn.* New York: Fawcett Columbine, 1994.

Pearson, Carol S. *Awakening the Heroes Within.* San Francisco: HarperSanFrancisco, 1991.

Perera, Sylvia Brinton. *Descent to the Goddess.* Toronto: Inner City Books, 1981.

Pipher, Mary. *Reviving Ophelia: Saving the Selves of Adolescent Girls.* New York: Putnam Publishing Group, 1994.

Sheehy, Gail. *New Passages.* New York: Random House, 1995.

Signell, Karen A. *Wisdom of the Heart.* New York: Bantam Books, 1990.

Stone, Hal, and Sidra Stone. *Embracing Your Inner Critic.* San Francisco: Harper Collins, 1993.

Stone, Merlin. *Ancient Mirrors of Womanhood.* Boston: Beacon Press, 1979.

Sussman, Linda. *The Speech of the Grail.* New York: Lindisfarne Press, 1995.

Tannen, Deborah. *You Just Don't Understand.* New York: William Morrow, Inc., 1990.

Thoele, Sue Patton. *The Woman's Book of Confidence.* Berkeley: Conari Press, 1997.

Tutuola, Amos. *The Village Witch Doctor and Other Stories.* London: Faber and Faber, 1990.

Walker, Barbara. *The Women's Encyclopedia of Myths and Secrets.* San Francisco: Harper & Row, 1983.

Wallis, Velma. *Two Old Women.* Seattle: Epicenter Press, 1993.

Walsch, Neale Donald. *Conversations with God.* New York: G. P. Putnam's Sons, 1996.

Woodman, Marion. *The Pregnant Virgin.* Toronto: Inner City Books, 1985.

Woodman, Marion, and Elinor Dickson. *Dancing in the Flames.* Boston: Shambhala Publications, 1996.

Credits

Grateful acknowledgment is made to the following poets and their publishers for permission to reprint copyrighted work.

Tina Michelle Datsko: "Momma and the Death Boutique" by Tina Michelle Datsko, © 1997, from her collection *Spiralling to the Light.* Reprinted with the author's permission.

Fiona O'Connell: "I come from a dark house" by Fiona O'Connell, © 1997. Reprinted with the author's permission.

May Sarton: "The Invocation to Kali, part 5," © 1971 by May Sarton, from *Collected Poems: 1930–1993* by May Sarton. Reprinted by permission of W. W. Norton & Company, Inc.

SOURCES OF ILLUSTRATIONS

Page ii: *Maidens and Crones, Vigeland Park, Oslo,* by Maureen Murdock. Black and white photograph, 1988.

Page 28: *Daughters of Demeter* by Joanne Battiste. Oil, 48 × 36 in., 1990. Reproduced by permission of the artist.

Page 66: *Grail Goddess* by Marti Glenn. Color collage, 8 × 12 in., 1996. Reproduced by permission of the artist.

Page 124: *Maskmaker* by Anna Pomaska. Black and white photograph taken at a Heroine's Journey Workshop, 5 × 7 in., 1992. Reproduced by permission of the artist.

Page 132: *The Three Tenses* by Joanne Battiste. Oil, 48 × 48 in., 1993. Reproduced by permission of the artist.